SAYINGS OF THE WISE

The Lion Classic Bible Series

SAYINGS
OF THE WISE

The Legacy of King Solomon

Foreword by Libby Purves
Introduction by Lawrence Boadt

A LION BOOK

Copyright © 1998 Lion Publishing

Published by
Lion Publishing plc
Sandy Lane West, Oxford, England
ISBN 0 7459 3888 4

First edition 1998
10 9 8 7 6 5 4 3 2 1 0

A catalogue record for this book is available
from the British Library

Typeset in 10/12 Berkeley Oldstyle
Printed and bound in Great Britain by
Caledonian International Book Manufacturing, Glasgow

Contents

ACKNOWLEDGMENTS

The introduction has been reprinted from *Reading the Old Testament* by Lawrence Boadt © 1984 by The Missionary Society of St Paul the Apostle in the State of New York. Used by permission of Paulist Press.

The text of 'Sayings of the Wise in Literature' has been selected from *A Dictionary of Biblical Tradition in English Literature*, edited by David Lyle Jeffrey, copyright © 1992 by permission of Wm B. Eerdmans Publishing Co.

The unabridged text of Proverbs and Ecclesiastes has been taken from the Authorized Version of the Bible (The King James Bible), the rights in which are vested in the Crown, by permission of the Crown's Patentee, Cambridge University Press.

Foreword

The books of Proverbs and Ecclesiastes rise like granite pillars from the gentle, lyrical rolling landscape of Psalms and the Song of Solomon. They tell no stories and offer no easy entertainment; their theme is wisdom and discretion and the long, narrow, difficult path through a life of pitfalls and temptations.

Always by the wise man's side, shadowing and sometimes replacing him, is the figure of the Fool: a doomed figure with his weakness, his stupid laughter crackling like thorns under a pot, his false sophistications and glittering empty sins. Along with the fool come a host of flatterers and deceivers, confidence tricksters and thieves and lechers, whose lips drip honey to lead the godly astray. The racket of the world is conveyed to us, the whole Vanity Fair of cackling distraction that shouts down the still small voice of calm. Only the Law and the Commandments provide a handrail along the cakewalk of life, and prevent the wise from tumbling headlong away from the right path and down to eternal death.

There is so much in these books that it has always been easy enough to misread them. Down Christian centuries, the Book of Proverbs probably fuelled more bigotry and terror than any other single book: children have been flogged and sinners ostracized all through our millennium for lacking the proper 'uprightness' and 'righteousness', or for being 'abominations before the Lord'. Prudent housekeeping, too, has been elevated by some sectarian interests after a reading of Proverbs 31 to stand right next to godliness, so that poverty itself becomes easy to identify as the sin of fecklessness. To some who took the Proverbs over-literally there must have been grave shock, in the New Testament, at being told to consider the lilies of the field who neither toil nor spin, and yet outshine Solomon. All in all, it would be easy for modern liberal sensitivities to misinterpret Proverbs as a somewhat disagreeable book.

Yet within it, in miniature, lies the rest of the Christian message: however righteous and prudent you may be, do not rob the poor, nor oppress the afflicted, nor indulge wrath. Read closely and there is, after all, no comfort here for the savagely self-righteous. Nor even for those prone to *schadenfreude*; chapter 24 makes it quite clear that rejoicing over the overthrow of the wicked is no part of wisdom.

Ecclesiastes, the great lament for the vanity of mere human endeavour, takes us further into wisdom. All the busyness of the good man, it tells us, will not avail him; all his work and study leads only to weariness, his art and laughter to madness, his love to sorrow and his life to death – unless God is in it. But as the great poem soars to its conclusion, the presence of God narrows the thousand strictures of the Preacher into the single simplicity of love, the first commandment. This is the end of the matter, says the prophet: fear God and keep his commandments, for this is the whole duty of man.

Few philosophers in the history of world thought have had the audacity to tell us, so plainly, what is the whole duty of man. But the power and complexity, the gentleness and strength of these two central books enforces respect. Their shape and their certainty speaks, if any scripture does, of a hand beyond the human author's.

It is odd to read them straight through, together: not least because so much of the two books is already lodged in hidden recesses of any literate mind. In both of them the poetry of the language and images are as rich as velvet tapestry and as harsh and terrible as a mountain range, and have sunk into Western consciousness over centuries: the sluggard turning on his bed like a door on its hinge, the man too idle to raise his hand to his mouth bearing food, the yawning grave and the barren womb, the woman whose price is above rubies, the due times and seasons, the bread cast upon the waters, the winds which go about and about, and the rivers which flow to the sea and cannot fill it. This is high and unforgettable art, striving to contain the uncontainable and map the moral universe. There has never been anything quite like it.

Libby Purves

INTRODUCTION

The Origins of Wisdom in Israel

Two major sources of Israel's interest in wisdom have been suggested by scholars. One is the *family*. The lists of proverbs, in particular, often dwell on the relations of parents and children, education, and moral instruction of the young. Here and there we find special evidence that fathers passed on golden nuggets of experience to their children. Deuteronomy 32:7 has, 'Ask your father and he will tell you, your elders and they will explain to you.' Proverbs 4:3 tells us, 'When I was a boy in my father's house, still tender and my mother's only child, he taught me and said, "Take my words to heart!"'

A second source would be *formal education*, especially in the royal administration. No one doubts that some education took place at home, but a professional class of wise men (and women) would require formal schools. Both Sumerian and Babylonian societies had schools where young boys learned how to be scribes to prepare them for careers in the royal court of the temples. The Bible itself indicates that Israel had its professional scribes like other nations: 1 Chronicles 27:32–33, Proverbs 25:1, and Sirach 38:24 – 39:11. There are indications that there was even a special class of wise counsellors that would be called on by the king (see 2 Samuel 15:31; 16:15 – 17:23; 1 Kings 12:6–7). In this, Israel followed the lead of other nations. The Bible often refers to the wise men of Edom and Egypt, Tyre and Assyria (e.g., Ezekiel 28:3–4; Jeremiah 49:7).

The king himself was considered to be the chief possessor of wisdom and judgment in the kingdom. David is called wise in 2 Samuel 14:20 and Solomon is famed for his wisdom. The first book of Kings 3–11 describes his reign as the model of the royal wisdom. He first asks God for wisdom above wealth or power (1 Kings 3) and then judges accurately and wisely in the case of two mothers claiming the same child (1 Kings 3). His temple and its beauty are considered the product of his wisdom (1 Kings 6–8), and the rulers of the far corners of the world, such as the queen of Sheba, come to hear his wisdom (1 Kings 10). Even his government of the country is portrayed as wisely ordered (1 Kings 4). The authors of his story have included a summary of Solomon's complete mastery of wisdom in 1 Kings 4:29–34:

> God gave Solomon wisdom and understanding and insights as numerous as the sand on the seashore. Solomon's wisdom was greater than all the wisdom of the East and of the Egyptians. He was wiser than any other person – wiser than Ethan the Ezrahite, and Heman, Calcol and Darda, the sons of Mahol. And his fame spread among the surrounding nations. He composed 3,000 proverbs and 1,005 songs. He described plants from the cedar of Lebanon down to the hyssop that grows on the walls. He taught about animals, birds, insects and fish. And people came from all parts of the world, sent by the kings of every nation who had heard of his wisdom, to listen to the wisdom of Solomon (In Hebrew, 1 Kings 5:9–14).

There is no complete statement in the Old Testament that actually says there were those who made their living as teachers of wisdom, but it is highly probable. A passing remark of Jeremiah places the wise on the same footing as priests and prophets:

> Then they said, 'Come, let us plot against Jeremiah, for the teaching of the law will not disappear from the priest, nor counsel from the wise, nor the word from the prophet' (Jeremiah 18:18).

Although it may be hard to prove exactly what a professional wise person did full-time, there are enough hints to put together a reasonable sketch. Wisdom sayings are directed to the educated, and education was usually socially restricted to the upper classes. The philosophy of life in wisdom books often reflects the concerns of people with money and those concerned with preserving political stability. The women mentioned in the book of Proverbs seem to have the leisure time for study. And in general, the concern with good speech, skill in writing, proper manners, and career planning, describes the ruling elite in Israel.

When David created an empire as large or larger than almost any other nation of his time, he had to find skilled diplomats, record-keepers and administrators quickly. This meant building a bureaucracy of scribes and political advisors from scratch. Under David and Solomon, a new burst of literary creativity took place, which included the first written story of Israel's faith, the J document. It also meant the founding of schools and the cultivation of wisdom as an art. In many early biblical passages, the word 'wise' is used for *skilled* carpenters and craftsmen. From the time of the Davidic monarchy on, the real skill of the wise was in the field of education and statecraft.

The Way of the Wise

Wisdom literature uses many distinctive literary forms such as the proverb, the riddle, and fables. These are especially common in Mesopotamian and Egyptian wisdom writings, but only the proverb is common in Hebrew. One or two fables occur in the Bible (Judges 9:8–15; Ezekiel 19:10–14), and a single, complete riddle (Judges 14:12–18), but none of these is in the Wisdom books. A few proverbs probably were recited as riddles, and most of these occur in a small collection of the 'Sayings of Agur' in Proverbs 30. One example is:

> There are three things that are never satisfied, four things that never say, 'Enough!': The grave, the barren womb, the land which never has enough water, and fire, which never says, 'Enough!' (Proverbs 30:15–16).

One can imagine the teacher asking the question, and the students reciting the four answers, or even adding other possible variations.

The proverb was an important element in Israelite wisdom, as it was in other ancient nations, for it distilled the lessons of the past, of human experience that seemed to be always the same, and it did so in a practical and clever manner with a little bit of the sermon about it for teaching purposes. This was ideally suited to a society which learned by memory and had only a few educated professionals who actually read books. One of the best illustrations of how effectively a society can live by proverbs is found in James Michener's novel, *The Source*. In chapter 7, 'In the Gymnasium', he has created a confrontation between a Jewish elder who seems to speak only in proverbs, and the educated, reasonable Greek governor of the small town. The traditional values of Jewish faith are able to withstand the allure of Greek culture, represented by the governor, because they have been so deeply absorbed by means of the proverbs that fill the mind of the Jewish elder.

The love for proverbs is a love for capturing the difficult problems of experience as well as the ordinariness of life in a new and interesting way. It helps to explain the other literary means adopted by the wise in Israel. They frequently used dialogue formats such as occur in the Book of Job, or question and answer exchanges, as in the Book of Ecclesiastes. Comparisons, allegories, and long images from nature are sometimes found, and the teachers always enjoyed rhetorical question for dramatic effect. These are all means of *instruction*. Above all, theirs is an educational outlook. And when not using one of the clever literary forms, they fell back on the straightforward lesson plan. Proverbs 1–9 is almost entirely written in such a teaching style, with twelve or thirteen separate lessons in all.

Because these proved to be such an effective method of educating people to both the traditional values and to moral reflection, the prophets often borrowed the techniques of the rhetorical question or the dialogue between God and people (or prophet and people) to convey their messages. Some prophets, such as Ezekiel, used the metaphor and parable as their favoured way of making a point (see Ezekiel 16, 17, 18, 19, 29, 30, 31, 32). But the prophet spoke directly to the covenant demands of Yahweh, while the wise concentrated on the wider questions of human experience and the problems of life. Yet they shared a common concern for the place of justice in society, personal responsibility, and the proper human response to divine command. Wisdom, prophecy and law may have followed different ways, but they had similar goals in the real life of the Israelite.

The Book of Proverbs

Solomon's reputation for wisdom was so great that Israel considered him the founder of their wisdom tradition. On the basis of 1 Kings 4:29–34 quoted above, he was believed to have been the author of the Book of Proverbs as well as The Song of Solomon and Ecclesiastes. Even the latest book of the Old Testament, the Wisdom of Solomon, is attributed to him. One charming legend in the Talmud guessed that Solomon had written the Song of Solomon in his lusty youth, Proverbs in his mature middle age, and the sceptical Ecclesiastes as an old man.

The Book of Proverbs contains a great number of sayings whose message is as old as the civilization of the Sumerians in 3000BC, and there is no reason why many of these could not have been collected under Solomon's command and formed into a book. But the present book also has many later additions. One group of proverbs in chapters 25–29 are attributed to Solomon but were not written down until two centuries later, in the time of King Hezekiah of Judah. Other small collections are labelled from other wise teachers and kings. Altogether, there are seven sections in the book:

(1) Chapters 1–9, labelled 'The Proverbs of Solomon, Son of David';
(2) Chapters 10–22, labelled 'Proverbs of Solomon';
(3) Chapters 22:17 – 24:22, labelled 'The Sayings of the Wise';
(4) Chapters 24:23–34, labelled 'Also the Sayings of the Wise';
(5) Chapters 25–29, labelled 'More Proverbs of Solomon, Copied by the Men of Hezekiah, King of Judah';
(6) Chapter 30, labelled 'The Sayings of Agur, son of Jakeh: An Oracle';
(7) Chapter 31, labelled 'The Sayings of King Lemuel: An Oracle'.

The identity of Agur and Lemuel cannot be known, but the third section seems to be an adaptation of the Egyptian collection of Amenemopet. All the sections are primarily collections of individual proverbs with no absolutely clear order that governs their arrangement, except within the first section, Proverbs 1–9. This is a larger, planned whole with a mixture of short proverbs and long instructions. It forms a prologue to the rest of Proverbs and an explanation of wisdom as a way of life. Proverbs 1:7 declares the basic theme: at the heart of all wisdom stands fear of the Lord. And the author repeats it again, at the end, in Proverbs 9:10: 'The fear of the Lord is the beginning of wisdom.' This fear of the Lord is true reverence and worship, and suggests obedience to the law of Yahweh as the way to find wisdom. At the same time, the author or authors of Proverbs 1–9 have borrowed many early themes known from Canaanite religion, such as the woman, Dame Folly, who seduces the young searcher after wisdom, in order to illustrate their points, but the overall view is that of the post-exilic period stress on law and wisdom as one. Thus this prologue was probably added to many earlier collections only at the final stage of development of the book.

The older proverbs found in the remaining chapters can be divided between pragmatic, secular, often materialistic advice, and the specifically religious reflections on the role of Yahweh as God of Israel. This is to be expected since the wisdom teachers were eager to include the wisdom of all peoples within the vision of Israel's faith. The overall purpose of learning proverbs is to master life. And the way to life is praised endlessly: 'The mouth of the just is a fountain of life' (Proverbs 10:11), and 'He who takes correction has a path to life' (Proverbs 10:17). Other topics that dominate the proverbs are:

(1) the relationship of parents and children especially in terms of respect for parents and discipline in education;
(2) the contrast between the just and the wicked in their behaviour;
(3) the value of good friends and a loving wife;
(4) the civic duties of honesty, generosity, justice, and integrity;
(5) personal mastery of passions and self-control, especially in sexual matters;
(6) proper use of speech, including knowing when not to speak;
(7) stewardship over wealth, prudence and hard work in planning for the future;
(8) manners and proper behaviour before superiors;
(9) the value of wisdom over foolish or careless behaviour.

These can be summed up in the words of a short maxim in Proverbs 13:20, 'Walk with wise men and you will become wise, but the friends of fools will come to a bad end.'

The nature of the proverb combines two somewhat opposed truths: it is evident to everyone as really so, but it is also ambiguous, and not always true in the same way in every case. Thus we can say, 'Absence makes the heart grow fonder', and 'Out of sight, out of mind', and mean both because different aspects of our experiences are brought out by each. So, too, Proverbs was not a boring book to our ancestors, but a treasure of practical wisdom which invited reflective thought and new discoveries of its meaning, especially in light of Yahweh's revelation of his word. It revealed the order of the world God had created and God's ultimate power over it: 'Man plans his way in his mind, but God controls his steps' (Proverbs 16:9).

The Book of Ecclesiastes

No one has ever challenged the Book of Ecclesiastes' right to the title of the most sceptical book in the Bible. Ecclesiastes, also called Qoheleth, has a unified approach to the value of wisdom: pessimism. While Proverbs sought to provide guidelines on what to do and what not to do, and confidently summed up the way to wisdom as 'fear of the Lord'. Ecclesiastes has its doubts whether such confidence has any basis in human experience. The author's theme song is sounded at the beginning and again at the end of the book, 'Vanity of vanities, all is vanity – and a striving after wind' (Ecclesiastes 1:2, 14; 12:8). Futility and emptiness result from the constant human search for the meaning of life. The author is particularly aware of the useless attempts to understand the mystery of divine purpose behind the order of the world as it is, the tragic finality of death, the reasons for success and failure, and the justice of rewards and punishment for good and evil behaviour. These are beyond the capabilities to discover.

The word Qoheleth is Hebrew for a 'preacher', 'head of the church assembly', or something similar, although no other example of the word exists in the Bible. The more traditional title of the book, Ecclesiastes, is nothing but a direct Greek translation of the Hebrew word. That the author was Solomon is implied by the first verse when it says Qoheleth was the son of David in Jerusalem, but cannot be taken as fact. The book shows the development of Israelite thought that comes after the exile, especially in its doubts about old answers and its attacks on the rational approaches of Greek thought that began to influence the Near East at that time.

The book has much in common with other wisdom literature, however. The author undertakes the investigation of experience at all levels, and asks questions about creation, justice, the wise versus the fool, just and unjust, and even quotes a large number of proverbs that he actually thinks will work in life. But certain things are clear to him that others have never allowed. While admitting that God does direct all things, he insists that we cannot know what God is doing or why, and so our proper human response is to enjoy what God gives us now and use it the best we can. As Ecclesiastes 5:17 puts it: 'Here is what I understand as good: it is well if a person eat, drink and enjoy all the fruits of work under the sun during the limited days that God gives to one's life, for this is a person's lot.' For Qoheleth, everything has its proper time: 'a time to be born and a time to die... a time to weep and a time to laugh' (Ecclesiastes 3:2–4), but the 'why' is known only to God and not to us. His advice to enjoy life as it is may not seem very religious, but he tempers it with warnings 'to fear God' (Ecclesiastes 5:6).

The Jewish rabbis fought a long time over whether the book was fit for the sacred canon of Scripture. The positive decision was made possible because Solomon was thought to be the author, and an editor added a pious afterword in Ecclesiastes 12:9–14 that summed up his message as 'fear God and keep his commandments' (Ecclesiastes 12:13). It was fortunate that they recognized its inspired nature, for it teaches the great gulf between the transcendent God and our human striving to understand and so control him. In the end, Ecclesiastes' message is one with that of Job – trust and surrender yourself to God's loving care even if you cannot know where it will lead.

Lawrence Boadt

SAYINGS OF THE WISE
IN LITERATURE

Quotations and Images

Quotations and Images

Bread upon the Waters

One of the many proverbs bequeathed by the book of Ecclesiastes to English literary usage is 'Cast thy bread upon the waters, for thou shalt find it after many days' (11:1). The injunction is to disinterested benevolence; as the *Glossa Ordinaria* cryptically notes, *'aptos fructificationi'* (*Patrologia Latina*, 113.1125). This is the sense employed by Mark Twain in *The Man That Corrupted Hadleyburg*, where Mrs Richards learns of the reward left for whoever had played Good Samaritan to the stranger, calling it 'a fortune for that kind man who set his bread afloat upon the waters!' In 20th-century literature the expression more often has ironic overtones, as when Shaw in *Village Wooing* uses it as a pretext for extravagant spending. O. Henry's card-sharp reflects on the returns of what he 'had cast upon the waters' – the deck he has marked in code ('The Man Higher Up'). And Somerset Maugham's narrator adverts to

> the philanthropist who with altruistic motives builds model dwellings for the poor and finds he has made a lucrative investment. He cannot prevent the satisfaction he feels in the ten per cent which rewards the bread he has cast upon the waters, but he has an awkward feeling that he detracts somewhat from the savour of his virtue. ('The Fall of Edward Barnard')

David L. Jeffrey
University of Ottawa

Dog Returneth to His Vomit

According to one of the common ancient Near Eastern proverbs recorded in the book of Proverbs, 'As a dog returneth to his vomit, so a fool returneth to his folly' (Proverbs 26:11; cf. 2 Peter 2:22). The classical application of this *mashal* appears in John Bunyan's *The Pilgrim's Progress*, as Hope explains the failure of Temporary to go along with Christian on his journey:

When the power of guilt weareth away, that which provoked them to be religious ceaseth. Wherefore they naturally turn to their own course again, even as we see a Dog that is sick of what he has eaten: he vomits and casts up all... but now when his sickness is over... he turns him about and licks up all; and so it is true which is written, The Dog is turned to his own vomit again.

Jonathan Edwards, in a similar echo of Puritan exegesis, tells how as a boy he lost his love for Christian faith and observance, and 'returned like a dog to his vomit, and went on in the ways of sin' (*Personal Narrative*). In spiritual autobiography and sermon literature of the 17th – 19th centuries this trope is commonly paired with 'backsliding'.

Manfred Siebald
Johannes Gutenberg Universität, Mainz, Germany

Go to the Ant, Thou Sluggard

The verse continues, '... consider her ways and be wise: Which having no guide, overseer, or ruler, provideth her meat in the summer and gathereth her food in the harvest. How long wilt thou sleep, O sluggard?' (Proverbs 6:6–9). This verse, generally adduced by patristic writers in condemnation of sloth, is what awakens Bunyan's Christian, asleep in his 'pleasant Arbour' on the 'Hill called Difficulty'. Milton uses it to argue against monarchical rule in *A Free Commonwealth*, modifying the translation to read 'having no prince, ruler, or lord'.

David L. Jeffrey
University of Ottawa

A Living Dog is Better than a Dead Lion

Death is the great leveller, according to Qoheleth. Hence, only for 'him that is joined to all the living there is hope: for a living dog is better than a dead lion' (Ecclesiastes 9:4). Thoreau says in his 'Conclusion' to *Walden* that grating protests that 'Americans, and moderns generally, are intellectual dwarfs compared to the ancients, or even the Elizabethan[s],' have little point: 'A living dog is better than a dead lion.' This Americanized version of Solomonic wisdom seems to be recognized by one of the characters in Somerset Maugham's *Cakes and Ale*: '"You don't know America as well as I do," he said, "they always prefer a live mouse to a dead lion. That's one of the reasons why I like America"' (chapter 24).

David L. Jeffrey
University of Ottawa

Of Making Many Books

Included in the summary of vanities in Ecclesiastes is the vanity of summarizing: 'And further, by these, my son, be admonished: of making many books there is no end; and much study is a weariness of the flesh' (12:12). The phrase has appealed to many a weary modern student, but in late antiquity and the Middle Ages when books were hand-copied, hence scarce and treasured, the verse was not so much commented upon as rationalized to these circumstances. Citing the passage, Hugh of St Victor interprets the injunction as a commending restraint: concerning books other than Scripture, including commentary on Scripture, 'it is necessary to use great discretion, lest what has been sought for our recovery may be found to stifle us... The number of books is infinite; do not pursue infinity! When no end is in sight, there can be no rest. Where there is no rest, there is no peace. Where there is no peace, God cannot dwell' (*Didascalicon*, 5.7). Richard de Bury in his *Philobiblion* relates the verse to the necessity of manual copying and remanufacture of books made necessary by decay: 'It is needful to replace the volumes that are worn out with age by fresh successors, that the perpetuity of which the individual is by nature incapable may be secured to the species; and hence it is that the Preacher says: *Of making many books there is no end*' (16.1). After the Reformation the observation of Matthew Henry that the Preacher implies that canonical Scripture 'is as much as God saw fit to give us, saw fit for us, and saw us fit for', becomes a commonplace among Puritan and Separatist writers. 'Let men write ever so many books for the conduct of human life, write till they have tired themselves with much study, they cannot give better instructions than those we have from the word of God' (*Commentary on the Whole Bible*, 4.1051).

The reading suggested by Shakespeare in *Love's Labour's Lost* is prompted by a suspicion of excessive intellectualism, a suspicion voiced by Berowne in his springtime counsel to the king of Navarre:

> Why, all delights are vain, but that most vain
> Which, with pain purchased, doth inherit pain:
> As, painfully to pore upon a book,
> To seek the light of truth, while truth the while
> Doth falsely blind the eyesight of his look. (1.1.72–76)

Berowne's words represent an acknowledgment that everything is 'fit in his place and time' (1.1.99; cf. Ecclesiastes 3:1), as well as a plea for common sense. In his *Areopagitica* Milton argues that one of the functions of God-given reason is to make a rational choice among available books: 'Solomon informs us, that much reading is a weariness of the flesh; but neither he, nor other inspired author, tells us that such or such reading is unlawful; yet, certainly had God thought good to limit us herein, it had been much more expedient to have told us what was unlawful, than what was wearisome.' Thomas Fuller in *The Holy and Profane State* begins his chapter 'Of Books' by averring: 'Solomon saith truly, "Of making many books there is no end", so insatiable is the thirst of men therein: as so endless is the desire of many in buying and reading them.' Elizabeth Barrett Browning cites the phrase conventionally in the first chapter of her *Aurora Leigh;* numerous other 19th- and 20th-century authors allude to 'a weariness of the flesh' – and not always in contexts which recall the first part of the verse. In this vein Hardy observes of one of his characters in *A Pair of Blue Eyes* that 'he saw nothing outside himself tonight; and what he saw within was a weariness of the flesh' (chapter 10).

David L. Jeffrey
University of Ottawa

Spare the Rod

The biblical phrase is from Proverbs: 'He that spareth his rod hateth his son: but he that loveth him chasteneth him betimes' (13:24). The more terse proverbial expression 'Spare the rod and spoil the child' is from Butler's *Hudibras* (2.1.843). If Washington Irving's Ichabod Crane thought of Butler's locution as a 'golden maxim' ('The Legend of Sleepy Hollow'), Mark Twain's Aunt Polly in *Tom Sawyer* repeats the popular assumption that it is itself a biblical text: 'I ain't doing my duty by that boy,' she says, 'and that's the Lord's truth, goodness. Spare the rod and spile the child, as the Good Book says' (chapter 1). One senses that the favour accorded the first phrase of the verse from Proverbs in Calvinistic circles acquired for successive generations in the Puritan tradition a legendary reinforcement. Hawthorne writes in *The Scarlet Letter* of how

> the discipline of the family in those days was of a far more rigid kind than now. The frown, the harsh rebuke, the frequent application of the rod, enjoined by Scriptural authority, were used, not merely in the way of punishment for actual offenses, but as a wholesome regimen for the growth and promotion of all childish virtues. (chapter 6)

And the narrator of Samuel Butler's *The Way of All Flesh* (1903) likewise observes of an earlier day: 'At that time it was universally admitted that to spare the rod was to spoil the child' (chapter 5).

David L. Jeffrey
University of Ottawa

To Everything... a Season

Qoheleth wrote that 'To every thing there is a season, and a time to every purpose under the heaven: A time to be born, and a time to die; a time to plant and a time to pluck up...' (Ecclesiastes 3:1–8). The phrase had become proverbial by Chaucer's era, as when Harry Bailey prods the quiescent Clerk into telling a tale:

> I trowe ye studie som sophyme;
> But Salomon seith, 'every thing hath tyme'.
> For Goddes sake, as beth of bettre cheere! (4.5–7)

David L. Jeffrey
University of Ottawa

Vanity of Vanities

'Vanity of vanities, saith the Preacher, vanity of vanities; all is vanity' (Ecclesiastes 1:2; Vulgate *'Vanitas vanitatem...'*). This most famous saying of the dyspeptic Qoheleth, commonly identified with Solomon, has become a tag or cliché in literature. It is the refrain, for example, in William Dunbar's 'Of the World is Vanitie', a 15th-century Scottish lyricist's denigration of 'this vaill of trubbil': *'Vanitas Vanitatum, et omnia Vanitas.'* Browning's corrupt bishop in 'The Bishop Orders his Tomb at St Praxed's Church' commences his deathbed request for an absurdly ornate and fabulously expensive tomb inscribed with 'Vanity, saith the preacher, vanity' – ironically an epitaph all too suitable. The concluding paragraph of Thackeray's *Vanity Fair*, appropriately enough, cites the 'Preacher': 'Ah, Vanitas vanitatem!' Melville writes in *Moby Dick* that 'the truest of all books is Solomon's, and Ecclesiastes is the fine hammered steel of woe. "All is vanity." ALL. This wilful world hath not got hold of unchristian Solomon's wisdom yet' (chapter 96).

The view that Solomon's book was a source of 'unchristian wisdom,' echoed in the late 19th century by scholars who detected (and admired) 'Hellenism' in it, as well as Stoic and Epicurean ideas (e.g., T. Tyler, *Ecclesiastes*, 1874; F.H. Plumptre, *Commentary on Ecclesiastes*, 1881), has since been largely discarded. It was, however, known and approved by Shaw (e.g., in *Man and Superman*), who liked to quote the phrase *vanitas vanitatem* from the author he called 'my friend Koheleth'. In his own *George Bernard Shaw*, Chesterton comments in response to his friend and rival: 'That all is vanity, that life is dust and love is ashes, these are frivolities, these are jokes that a Catholic can afford to utter' ('The Critic').

David L. Jeffrey
University of Ottawa

Virtuous Woman

Proverbs 31:10–31, an acrostic poem in praise of female virtue, constitutes an extension of the sayings of Lemuel (perhaps an Arab king) which he attributes in verses 1–9 to his mother. The passage may thus provide a rare instance of non-Hebrew and female authorship of Scripture. Rabbinic commentary prefers to see 'Lemuel' (Hebrew = 'Belonging to God') as a nom de plume or attribute name for Solomon, and does not comment on the maternal source of the 'wisdom' (Targum Sheni 1.2.4; Shir ha Shirim Rabbah 1.1). The passage describes the 'strong woman' (Vulgate *mulier fortis*) as of inestimable value to her husband and children; her price is 'above rubies'. She is a spinner of wool and flax, an effective and prosperous businesswoman, a benevolent force in society, and a disciple of wisdom.

Medieval commentary on this passage, along with an analogue in Ecclesiasticus 26:1–24, is extensive. Among the most important elaborations are the *Liber Consolationis et Consilii* of Albert of Brescia, which Chaucer paraphrases closely in his characterization of Dame Prudence in *The Tale of Melibee* (*Canterbury Tales*, 7.1064ff.). The *mulier fortis* is here Lady Wisdom herself, a figure from the earlier chapters of Proverbs, the proper object of a young ruler's highest affection. Other commentators were to identify the *mulier fortis* allegorically with the Church (e.g., *Glossa Ordinaria*, *Patrologia Latina*, 113.1114–16) or Bride of Christ in whom Christ may safely trust as both faithful and fruitful unto good works. Applied literally, the description becomes a kind of medieval stereotype for womanly virtue, as in John Gower's *Vox Clamantis*, where the text is invoked to explain how the character of good and bad women affects men (5.6). Chaucer appears to have drawn heavily on this passage for his sympathetic characterization of the wife in *The Shipman's Tale;* his Wife of Bath, also a spinner of flax and wool and a businesswoman of some enterprise, is a kind of parody of the *mulier fortis* (Proverbs 31:10 is found as a gloss on line 689 of the Prologue to her tale in some manuscripts of *The Canterbury Tales*). Bunyan's portrait of Prudence and Christiana in part 2 of *Pilgrim's Progress* is indebted to Proverbs 31. In Hardy's *Tess of the D'Urbervilles* (chapter 39), when Angel Clare returns home alone and without explanation three weeks after his ill-fated marriage to Tess, his father chooses to read 'The words of King Lemuel' to honour the absent bride. Mrs Clare's sense of the aptness of the passage in describing Tess underscores Angel's confusion and torment:

The perfect woman, you see, was a working woman; not an idler; not a fine lady; but one who used her hands and her head and her heart for the good of others. 'Her children arise up and call her blessed; her husband also, and he praiseth her. Many daughters have done virtuously, but she excelleth them all.' Well, I wish I could have seen her, Angel. Since she is pure and chaste she would have been refined enough for me.

The passage is extensively cited throughout Mulock's *John Halifax*, where it is usually applied to the character of Mrs Halifax (e.g., chapters 22, 30). In Somerset Maugham's *The Mixture as Before*, 'People envied Harenger the possession of her as they envied nothing else that he had. She was worth her weight in gold. Her price was above rubies. Richard Harenger beamed with self-complacency when they praised her' ('The Treasure'). One of the novels of Louis Bromfield, *The Good Woman* (1927), concerns the relationship between a dominated son and his missionary mother, and there are oblique references in Bertolt Brecht's *Good Woman of Setzuan* and *Mother Courage* (1941).

David L. Jeffrey
University of Ottawa

Whatsoever Thy Hand Findeth to Do

It is a maxim of Qoheleth that 'Whatsoever thy hand findeth to do, do it with thy might; for there is no work, nor device, nor knowledge, nor wisdom, in the grave, whither thou goest' (Ecclesiastes 9:10). Christian exegesis, particularly after Calvin and among the Puritans, makes this an injunction to Christian stewardship. Carlyle concludes 'The Everlasting Yea' section of his *Sartor Resartus* by saying: 'Produce! Produce! Were it but the pitifullest, infinitesimal fraction of a product, produce it, in God's name!... Up, Up! "Whatsoever thy hand findeth to do, do it with thy whole might"' (2.9).

David L. Jeffrey
University of Ottawa

Whole Duty of Man

At the end of his book, Qoheleth ('the Preacher') sums up his counsel: 'Let us hear the conclusion of the whole matter: Fear God and keep his commandments: for this is the whole duty of man' (Ecclesiastes 12:13). St Augustine observes of this passage (in which the Vulgate reads only *hoc est enim omnis homo;* KJV adds 'duty') that 'whosoever has real existence is this, a keeper of God's commandments; and he who is not this, is nothing' (*De civitate Dei* 20.3). Matthew Henry call this verse 'the summary of religion', adding, 'In vain do we pretend to fear God if we do not make a conscience of our duty to him' (*Commentary* 4.1052).

This emphasis on 'obedience', 'conscience', and 'duty' as the epitome of true religion finds an enormously popular expression in *The Whole Duty of Man* (1658), an anonymous work (possibly by Richard Allestree) which for more than a century had an undisputed place alongside the Prayer Book as a practical church guide to social conduct and responsibility. Although largely conventional in its religious precepts, this work was directed against nonconformity as well as the aspirations of those in the lower and middle classes – teaching that ordinary persons, like children, should 'order themselves lowely and reverently to all their betters' (293). Prior to his conversion John Wesley held this work in high esteem; after it, in light of his concerns for the social outworking of the gospel, he publicly rejected it in terms akin to those of William Cowper, who described it as 'a repository of self-righteousness and pharisaical lumber'. It is often this book rather than the passage in Ecclesiastes which is alluded to by English writers, as is the case with Carlyle in *Sartor Resartus*, where Professor Teufelsdröckh wants to argue the 'Everlasting Yea': 'If Fichte's *Wissenschaftslehre* be, "to a certain extent, Applied Christianity", surely to a still greater extent, so is this. We have not a Whole Duty of Man, yet a Half Duty, namely the Passive half: could we but do it, as we can demonstrate it!' (2.9).

David L. Jeffrey
University of Ottawa

SAYINGS OF THE WISE

Part One

The Book of Proverbs

PROLOGUE
Proverbs 1:1–7

The proverbs of Solomon the son of David, king of Israel;

To know wisdom and instruction;
  to perceive the words of understanding;
To receive the instruction of wisdom,
  justice, and judgment, and equity;
To give subtilty to the simple,
  to the young man knowledge and discretion.
A wise man will hear, and will increase learning;
  and a man of understanding shall attain unto wise counsels:
To understand a proverb, and the interpretation;
  the words of the wise, and their dark sayings.

The fear of the Lord is the beginning of knowledge:
  but fools despise wisdom and instruction.

THE VOICE OF WISDOM
Proverbs 1:8 – 9:18

My son, hear the instruction of thy father,
  and forsake not the law of thy mother:
For they shall be an ornament of grace unto thy head,
  and chains about thy neck.

My son, if sinners entice thee, consent thou not.
If they say, Come with us, let us lay wait for blood,
  let us lurk privily for the innocent without cause:

Let us swallow them up alive as the grave;
  and whole, as those that go down into the pit:
We shall find all precious substance,
  we shall fill our houses with spoil:
Cast in thy lot among us;
  let us all have one purse:
My son, walk not thou in the way with them;
  refrain thy foot from their path:
For their feet run to evil, and make haste to shed blood.
Surely in vain the net is spread in the sight of any bird.
And they lay wait for their own blood;
  they lurk privily for their own lives.
So are the ways of every one that is greedy of gain;
  which taketh away the life of the owners thereof.

Wisdom crieth without; she uttereth her voice in the streets: she crieth in the chief place of concourse, in the openings of the gates: in the city she uttereth her words, saying:

How long, ye simple ones, will ye love simplicity?
  and the scorners delight in their scorning,
  and fools hate knowledge?
Turn you at my reproof: behold,
  I will pour out my spirit unto you,
  I will make known my words unto you.
Because I have called, and ye refused;
  I have stretched out my hand, and no man regarded;
But ye have set at nought all my counsel,
  and would none of my reproof:
I also will laugh at your calamity;
  I will mock when your fear cometh;
When your fear cometh as desolation,
  and your destruction cometh as a whirlwind;
  when distress and anguish cometh upon you.

Then shall they call upon me, but I will not answer;
  they shall seek me early, but they shall not find me:
For that they hated knowledge, and did not choose
  the fear of the Lord:

They would none of my counsel:
　　they despised all my reproof.
Therefore shall they eat of the fruit of their own way,
　　and be filled with their own devices.
For the turning away of the simple shall slay them,
　　and the prosperity of fools shall destroy them.
But whoso hearkeneth unto me shall dwell safely,
　　and shall be quiet from fear of evil.

My son, if thou wilt receive my words,
　　and hide my commandments with thee;
So that thou incline thine ear unto wisdom,
　　and apply thine heart to understanding;
Yea, if thou criest after knowledge,
　　and liftest up thy voice for understanding;
If thou seekest her as silver,
　　and searchest for her as for hid treasures;
Then shalt thou understand the fear of the Lord,
　　and find the knowledge of God.
For the Lord giveth wisdom:
　　out of his mouth cometh knowledge and understanding.
He layeth up sound wisdom for the righteous:
　　he is a buckler to them that walk uprightly.
He keepeth the paths of judgment,
　　and preserveth the way of his saints.

Then shalt thou understand righteousness,
　　and judgment, and equity; yea, every good path.
When wisdom entereth into thine heart,
　　and knowledge is pleasant unto thy soul;
Discretion shall preserve thee,
　　understanding shall keep thee:
To deliver thee from the way of the evil man,
　　from the man that speaketh froward things;
Who leave the paths of uprightness,
　　to walk in the ways of darkness;
Who rejoice to do evil, and delight
　　in the frowardness of the wicked;

Whose ways are crooked,
  and they froward in their paths:
To deliver thee from the strange woman,
  even from the stranger which flattereth with her words;
Which forsaketh the guide of her youth,
  and forgetteth the covenant of her God.
For her house inclineth unto death,
  and her paths unto the dead.
None that go unto her return again,
  neither take they hold of the paths of life.

That thou mayest walk in the way of good men,
  and keep the paths of the righteous.
For the upright shall dwell in the land,
  and the perfect shall remain in it.
But the wicked shall be cut off from the earth,
  and the transgressors shall be rooted out of it.

My son, forget not my law;
  but let thine heart keep my commandments:
For length of days, and long life, and peace,
  shall they add to thee.

Let not mercy and truth forsake thee:
  bind them about thy neck;
  write them upon the table of thine heart:
So shalt thou find favour and good understanding
  in the sight of God and man.

Trust in the Lord with all thine heart;
  and lean not unto thine own understanding.
In all thy ways acknowledge him,
  and he shall direct thy paths.

Be not wise in thine own eyes:
  fear the Lord, and depart from evil.
It shall be health to thy navel, and marrow to thy bones.

Honour the Lord with thy substance,
  and with the firstfruits of all thine increase:

So shall thy barns be filled with plenty,
and thy presses shall burst out with new wine.

My son, despise not the chastening of the Lord;
neither be weary of his correction:
For whom the Lord loveth he correcteth;
even as a father the son in whom he delighteth.

Happy is the man that findeth wisdom,
and the man that getteth understanding.
For the merchandise of it is better than the merchandise of silver,
and the gain thereof than fine gold.
She is more precious than rubies: and all the things
thou canst desire are not to be compared unto her.
Length of days is in her right hand;
and in her left hand riches and honour.
Her ways are ways of pleasantness,
and all her paths are peace.
She is a tree of life to them that lay hold upon her:
and happy is every one that retaineth her.

The Lord by wisdom hath founded the earth;
by understanding hath he established the heavens.
By his knowledge the depths are broken up,
and the clouds drop down the dew.

My son, let not them depart from thine eyes:
keep sound wisdom and discretion:
So shall they be life unto thy soul,
and grace to thy neck.
Then shalt thou walk in thy way safely,
and thy foot shall not stumble.
When thou liest down, thou shalt not be afraid:
yea, thou shalt lie down, and thy sleep shall be sweet.
Be not afraid of sudden fear,
neither of the desolation of the wicked, when it cometh.
For the Lord shall be thy confidence,
and shall keep thy foot from being taken.

Withhold not good from them to whom it is due,
    when it is in the power of thine hand to do it.
Say not unto thy neighbour,
    Go, and come again,
and to morrow I will give;
    when thou hast it by thee.
Devise not evil against thy neighbour,
    seeing he dwelleth securely by thee.
Strive not with a man without cause,
    if he have done thee no harm.

Envy thou not the oppressor,
    and choose none of his ways.
For the froward is abomination to the Lord:
    but his secret is with the righteous.

The curse of the Lord is in the house of the wicked:
    but he blesseth the habitation of the just.
Surely he scorneth the scorners:
    but he giveth grace unto the lowly.
The wise shall inherit glory:
    but shame shall be the promotion of fools.

Hear, ye children, the instruction of a father,
    and attend to know understanding.
For I give you good doctrine, forsake ye not my law.
For I was my father's son,
    tender and only beloved in the sight of my mother.
He taught me also, and said unto me,
Let thine heart retain my words:
    keep my commandments, and live.
Get wisdom, get understanding: forget it not;
    neither decline from the words of my mouth.
Forsake her not, and she shall preserve thee:
    love her, and she shall keep thee.
Wisdom is the principal thing; therefore get wisdom:
    and with all thy getting get understanding.
Exalt her, and she shall promote thee:
    she shall bring thee to honour, when thou dost embrace her.

She shall give to thine head an ornament of grace:
a crown of glory shall she deliver to thee.

Hear, O my son, and receive my sayings;
and the years of thy life shall be many.
I have taught thee in the way of wisdom;
I have led thee in right paths.
When thou goest, thy steps shall not be straitened;
and when thou runnest, thou shalt not stumble.
Take fast hold of instruction; let her not go:
keep her; for she is thy life.
Enter not into the path of the wicked,
and go not in the way of evil men.
Avoid it, pass not by it, turn from it, and pass away.
For they sleep not, except they have done mischief;
and their sleep is taken away, unless they cause some to fall.
For they eat the bread of wickedness,
and drink the wine of violence.

But the path of the just is as the shining light,
that shineth more and more unto the perfect day.
The way of the wicked is as darkness:
they know not at what they stumble.

My son, attend to my words;
incline thine ear unto my sayings.
Let them not depart from thine eyes;
keep them in the midst of thine heart.
For they are life unto those that find them,
and health to all their flesh.
Keep thy heart with all diligence;
for out of it are the issues of life.
Put away from thee a froward mouth,
and perverse lips put far from thee.
Let thine eyes look right on,
and let thine eyelids look straight before thee.
Ponder the path of thy feet,
and let all thy ways be established.

Turn not to the right hand nor to the left:
  remove thy foot from evil.

My son, attend unto my wisdom,
  and bow thine ear to my understanding:
That thou mayest regard discretion,
  and that thy lips may keep knowledge.
For the lips of a strange woman drop as an honeycomb,
  and her mouth is smoother than oil:
But her end is bitter as wormwood,
  sharp as a twoedged sword.
Her feet go down to death;
  her steps take hold on hell.
Lest thou shouldest ponder the path of life,
  her ways are moveable,
    that thou canst not know them.

Hear me now therefore, O ye children,
  and depart not from the words of my mouth.
Remove thy way far from her,
  and come not nigh the door of her house:
Lest thou give thine honour unto others,
  and thy years unto the cruel:
Lest strangers be filled with thy wealth;
  and thy labours be in the house of a stranger;
And thou mourn at the last,
  when thy flesh and thy body are consumed,
And say, How have I hated instruction,
  and my heart despised reproof;
And have not obeyed the voice of my teachers,
  nor inclined mine ear to them that instructed me!
I was almost in all evil
  in the midst of the congregation and assembly.

Drink waters out of thine own cistern,
  and running waters out of thine own well.
Let thy fountains be dispersed abroad,
  and rivers of waters in the streets.

Let them be only thine own,
     and not strangers' with thee.
Let thy fountain be blessed:
     and rejoice with the wife of thy youth.
Let her be as the loving hind and pleasant roe;
     let her breasts satisfy thee at all times;
     and be thou ravished always with her love.
And why wilt thou, my son, be ravished with a strange woman,
     and embrace the bosom of a stranger?

For the ways of man are before the eyes of the Lord,
     and he pondereth all his goings.
His own iniquities shall take the wicked himself,
     and he shall be holden with the cords of his sins.
He shall die without instruction;
     and in the greatness of his folly he shall go astray.

My son, if thou be surety for thy friend,
     if thou hast stricken thy hand with a stranger,
Thou art snared with the words of thy mouth,
     thou art taken with the words of thy mouth.
Do this now, my son, and deliver thyself,
     when thou art come into the hand of thy friend;
     go, humble thyself, and make sure thy friend.
Give not sleep to thine eyes, nor slumber to thine eyelids.
Deliver thyself as a roe from the hand of the hunter,
     and as a bird from the hand of the fowler.

Go to the ant, thou sluggard;
     consider her ways, and be wise:
Which having no guide, overseer, or ruler,
Provideth her meat in the summer,
     and gathereth her food in the harvest.
How long wilt thou sleep, O sluggard?
     when wilt thou arise out of thy sleep?
Yet a little sleep, a little slumber,
     a little folding of the hands to sleep:
So shall thy poverty come as one that travelleth,
     and thy want as an armed man.

A naughty person, a wicked man,
    walketh with a froward mouth.
He winketh with his eyes, he speaketh with his feet,
    he teacheth with his fingers;
Frowardness is in his heart,
    he deviseth mischief continually; he soweth discord.
Therefore shall his calamity come suddenly;
    suddenly shall he be broken without remedy.

These six things doth the Lord hate:
    yea, seven are an abomination unto him:
A proud look, a lying tongue,
    and hands that shed innocent blood,
An heart that deviseth wicked imaginations,
    feet that be swift in running to mischief,
A false witness that speaketh lies,
    and he that soweth discord among brethren.

My son, keep thy father's commandment,
    and forsake not the law of thy mother:
Bind them continually upon thine heart,
    and tie them about thy neck.
When thou goest, it shall lead thee;
    when thou sleepest, it shall keep thee;
    and when thou awakest, it shall talk with thee.
For the commandment is a lamp; and the law is light;
    and reproofs of instruction are the way of life:
To keep thee from the evil woman,
    from the flattery of the tongue of a strange woman.
Lust not after her beauty in thine heart;
    neither let her take thee with her eyelids.
For by means of a whorish woman
    a man is brought to a piece of bread:
    and the adulteress will hunt for the precious life.
Can a man take fire in his bosom,
    and his clothes not be burned?
Can one go upon hot coals,
    and his feet not be burned?

So he that goeth in to his neighbour's wife;
    whosoever toucheth her shall not be innocent.

Men do not despise a thief,
    if he steal to satisfy his soul when he is hungry;
But if he be found, he shall restore sevenfold;
    he shall give all the substance of his house.
But whoso committeth adultery with a woman
    lacketh understanding:
    he that doeth it destroyeth his own soul.
A wound and dishonour shall he get;
    and his reproach shall not be wiped away.
For jealousy is the rage of a man:
    therefore he will not spare in the day of vengeance.
He will not regard any ransom;
    neither will he rest content, though thou givest many gifts.

My son, keep my words,
    and lay up my commandments with thee.
Keep my commandments, and live;
    and my law as the apple of thine eye.
Bind them upon thy fingers,
    write them upon the table of thine heart.
Say unto wisdom, Thou art my sister;
    and call understanding thy kinswoman:
That they may keep thee from the strange woman,
    from the stranger which flattereth with her words.

For at the window of my house
    I looked through my casement,
And beheld among the simple ones,
I discerned among the youths,
    a young man void of understanding,
Passing through the street near her corner;
    and he went the way to her house,
In the twilight, in the evening,
    in the black and dark night:
And, behold, there met him a woman
    with the attire of an harlot, and subtil of heart.

(She is loud and stubborn;
    her feet abide not in her house:
Now is she without, now in the streets,
    and lieth in wait at every corner.)
So she caught him, and kissed him,
    and with an impudent face said unto him,
I have peace offerings with me;
    this day have I payed my vows.
Therefore came I forth to meet thee,
    diligently to seek thy face, and I have found thee.
I have decked my bed with coverings of tapestry,
    with carved works, with fine linen of Egypt.
I have perfumed my bed with myrrh, aloes, and cinnamon.
Come, let us take our fill of love until the morning:
    let us solace ourselves with loves.
For the goodman is not at home,
    he is gone a long journey:
He hath taken a bag of money with him,
    and will come home at the day appointed.

With her much fair speech she caused him to yield,
    with the flattering of her lips she forced him.
He goeth after her straightway, as an ox goeth to the slaughter,
    or as a fool to the correction of the stocks;
Till a dart strike through his liver; as a bird hasteth to the snare,
    and knoweth not that it is for his life.

Hearken unto me now therefore, O ye children,
    and attend to the words of my mouth.
Let not thine heart decline to her ways,
    go not astray in her paths.
For she hath cast down many wounded:
    yea, many strong men have been slain by her.
Her house is the way to hell,
    going down to the chambers of death.

Doth not wisdom cry?
    and understanding put forth her voice?

She standeth in the top of high places,
>by the way in the places of the paths.
She crieth at the gates, at the entry of the city,
>at the coming in at the doors.
Unto you, O men, I call;
>and my voice is to the sons of man.
O ye simple, understand wisdom:
>and, ye fools, be ye of an understanding heart.
Hear; for I will speak of excellent things;
>and the opening of my lips shall be right things.
For my mouth shall speak truth;
>and wickedness is an abomination to my lips.
All the words of my mouth are in righteousness;
>there is nothing froward or perverse in them.
They are all plain to him that understandeth,
>and right to them that find knowledge.
Receive my instruction, and not silver;
>and knowledge rather than choice gold.
For wisdom is better than rubies;
>and all the things that may be desired
>are not to be compared to it.

I wisdom dwell with prudence,
>and find out knowledge of witty inventions.
The fear of the Lord is to hate evil:
>pride, and arrogancy, and the evil way,
>and the froward mouth, do I hate.
Counsel is mine, and sound wisdom:
>I am understanding; I have strength.
By me kings reign,
>and princes decree justice.
By me princes rule, and nobles,
>even all the judges of the earth.
I love them that love me;
>and those that seek me early shall find me.
Riches and honour are with me;
>yea, durable riches and righteousness.

My fruit is better than gold, yea, than fine gold;
  and my revenue than choice silver.
I lead in the way of righteousness,
  in the midst of the paths of judgment:
That I may cause those that love me to inherit substance;
  and I will fill their treasures.

The Lord possessed me in the beginning of his way,
  before his works of old.
I was set up from everlasting,
  from the beginning, or ever the earth was.
When there were no depths, I was brought forth;
  when there were no fountains abounding with water.
Before the mountains were settled,
  before the hills was I brought forth:
While as yet he had not made the earth, nor the fields,
  nor the highest part of the dust of the world.
When he prepared the heavens, I was there:
  when he set a compass upon the face of the depth:
When he established the clouds above:
  when he strengthened the fountains of the deep:
When he gave to the sea his decree,
  that the waters should not pass his commandment:
  when he appointed the foundations of the earth:
Then I was by him, as one brought up with him:
  and I was daily his delight, rejoicing always before him;
Rejoicing in the habitable part of his earth;
  and my delights were with the sons of men.

Now therefore hearken unto me, O ye children:
  for blessed are they that keep my ways.
Hear instruction, and be wise, and refuse it not.
Blessed is the man that heareth me,
  watching daily at my gates, waiting at the posts of my doors.
For whoso findeth me findeth life,
  and shall obtain favour of the Lord.
But he that sinneth against me wrongeth his own soul:
  all they that hate me love death.

Wisdom hath builded her house,
   she hath hewn out her seven pillars:
She hath killed her beasts; she hath mingled her wine;
   she hath also furnished her table.
She hath sent forth her maidens:
   she crieth upon the highest places of the city,
Whoso is simple, let him turn in hither:
   as for him that wanteth understanding, she saith to him,
Come, eat of my bread,
   and drink of the wine which I have mingled.
Forsake the foolish, and live;
   and go in the way of understanding.

He that reproveth a scorner getteth to himself shame:
   and he that rebuketh a wicked man getteth himself a blot.
Reprove not a scorner, lest he hate thee:
   rebuke a wise man, and he will love thee.
Give instruction to a wise man, and he will be yet wiser:
   teach a just man, and he will increase in learning.

The fear of the Lord is the beginning of wisdom:
   and the knowledge of the holy is understanding.
For by me thy days shall be multiplied,
   and the years of thy life shall be increased.
If thou be wise, thou shalt be wise for thyself:
   but if thou scornest, thou alone shalt bear it.

A foolish woman is clamorous:
   she is simple, and knoweth nothing.
For she sitteth at the door of her house,
   on a seat in the high places of the city,
To call passengers who go right on their ways:
Whoso is simple, let him turn in hither:
   and as for him that wanteth understanding, she saith to him,
Stolen waters are sweet,
   and bread eaten in secret is pleasant.
But he knoweth not that the dead are there;
   and that her guests are in the depths of hell.

PROVERBS OF SOLOMON
Proverbs 10:1 – 22:16

The proverbs of Solomon.

A wise son maketh a glad father:
but a foolish son is the heaviness of his mother.
Treasures of wickedness profit nothing:
but righteousness delivereth from death.

The Lord will not suffer the soul of the righteous to famish:
but he casteth away the substance of the wicked.

He becometh poor that dealeth with a slack hand:
but the hand of the diligent maketh rich.

He that gathereth in summer is a wise son:
but he that sleepeth in harvest is a son that causeth shame.

Blessings are upon the head of the just:
but violence covereth the mouth of the wicked.

The memory of the just is blessed:
but the name of the wicked shall rot.

The wise in heart will receive commandments:
but a prating fool shall fall.

He that walketh uprightly walketh surely:
but he that perverteth his ways shall be known.

He that winketh with the eye causeth sorrow:
but a prating fool shall fall.

The mouth of a righteous man is a well of life:
but violence covereth the mouth of the wicked.

Hatred stirreth up strifes:
but love covereth all sins.

In the lips of him that hath understanding wisdom is found:
but a rod is for the back of him that is void of understanding.

Wise men lay up knowledge:
    but the mouth of the foolish is near destruction.

The rich man's wealth is his strong city:
    the destruction of the poor is their poverty.

The labour of the righteous tendeth to life:
    the fruit of the wicked to sin.

He is in the way of life that keepeth instruction:
    but he that refuseth reproof erreth.

He that hideth hatred with lying lips,
    and he that uttereth a slander, is a fool.

In the multitude of words there wanteth not sin:
    but he that refraineth his lips is wise.

The tongue of the just is as choice silver:
    the heart of the wicked is little worth.

The lips of the righteous feed many:
    but fools die for want of wisdom.

The blessing of the Lord, it maketh rich,
    and he addeth no sorrow with it.

It is as sport to a fool to do mischief:
    but a man of understanding hath wisdom.

The fear of the wicked, it shall come upon him:
    but the desire of the righteous shall be granted.

As the whirlwind passeth, so is the wicked no more:
    but the righteous is an everlasting foundation.

As vinegar to the teeth, and as smoke to the eyes,
    so is the sluggard to them that send him.

The fear of the Lord prolongeth days:
    but the years of the wicked shall be shortened.

The hope of the righteous shall be gladness:
    but the expectation of the wicked shall perish.

The way of the Lord is strength to the upright:
　　but destruction shall be to the workers of iniquity.

The righteous shall never be removed:
　　but the wicked shall not inhabit the earth.

The mouth of the just bringeth forth wisdom:
　　but the froward tongue shall be cut out.

The lips of the righteous know what is acceptable:
　　but the mouth of the wicked speaketh frowardness.

A false balance is abomination to the Lord:
　　but a just weight is his delight.

When pride cometh, then cometh shame:
　　but with the lowly is wisdom.

The integrity of the upright shall guide them:
　　but the perverseness of transgressors shall destroy them.

Riches profit not in the day of wrath:
　　but righteousness delivereth from death.

The righteousness of the perfect shall direct his way:
　　but the wicked shall fall by his own wickedness.

The righteousness of the upright shall deliver them:
　　but transgressors shall be taken in their own naughtiness.

When a wicked man dieth, his expectation shall perish:
　　and the hope of unjust men perisheth.

The righteous is delivered out of trouble,
　　and the wicked cometh in his stead.

An hypocrite with his mouth destroyeth his neighbour:
　　but through knowledge shall the just be delivered.

When it goeth well with the righteous, the city rejoiceth:
　　and when the wicked perish, there is shouting.

By the blessing of the upright the city is exalted:
　　but it is overthrown by the mouth of the wicked.

He that is void of wisdom despiseth his neighbour:
    but a man of understanding holdeth his peace.

A talebearer revealeth secrets:
    but he that is of a faithful spirit concealeth the matter.

Where no counsel is, the people fall:
    but in the multitude of counsellors there is safety.

He that is surety for a stranger shall smart for it:
    and he that hateth suretiship is sure.

A gracious woman retaineth honour:
    and strong men retain riches.

The merciful man doeth good to his own soul:
    but he that is cruel troubleth his own flesh.

The wicked worketh a deceitful work:
    but to him that soweth righteousness shall be a sure reward.

As righteousness tendeth to life:
    so he that pursueth evil pursueth it to his own death.

They that are of a froward heart are abomination to the Lord:
    but such as are upright in their way are his delight.

Though hand join in hand, the wicked shall not be unpunished:
    but the seed of the righteous shall be delivered.

As a jewel of gold in a swine's snout,
    so is a fair woman which is without discretion.

The desire of the righteous is only good:
    but the expectation of the wicked is wrath.

There is that scattereth, and yet increaseth;
    and there is that withholdeth more than is meet,
    but it tendeth to poverty.

The liberal soul shall be made fat:
    and he that watereth shall be watered also himself.

He that withholdeth corn, the people shall curse him:
    but blessing shall be upon the head of him that selleth it.

He that diligently seeketh good procureth favour:
  but he that seeketh mischief, it shall come unto him.

He that trusteth in his riches shall fall:
  but the righteous shall flourish as a branch.

He that troubleth his own house shall inherit the wind:
  and the fool shall be servant to the wise of heart.

The fruit of the righteous is a tree of life;
  and he that winneth souls is wise.

Behold, the righteous shall be recompensed in the earth:
  much more the wicked and the sinner.

Whoso loveth instruction loveth knowledge:
  but he that hateth reproof is brutish.

A good man obtaineth favour of the Lord:
  but a man of wicked devices will he condemn.

A man shall not be established by wickedness:
  but the root of the righteous shall not be moved.

A virtuous woman is a crown to her husband:
  but she that maketh ashamed is as rottenness in his bones.

The thoughts of the righteous are right:
  but the counsels of the wicked are deceit.

The words of the wicked are to lie in wait for blood:
  but the mouth of the upright shall deliver them.

The wicked are overthrown, and are not:
  but the house of the righteous shall stand.

A man shall be commended according to his wisdom:
  but he that is of a perverse heart shall be despised.

He that is despised, and hath a servant,
  is better than he that honoureth himself, and lacketh bread.

A righteous man regardeth the life of his beast:
  but the tender mercies of the wicked are cruel.

He that tilleth his land shall be satisfied with bread:
    but he that followeth vain persons is void of understanding.

The wicked desireth the net of evil men:
    but the root of the righteous yieldeth fruit.

The wicked is snared by the transgression of his lips:
    but the just shall come out of trouble.

A man shall be satisfied with good by the fruit of his mouth:
    and the recompence of a man's hands
    shall be rendered unto him.

The way of a fool is right in his own eyes:
    but he that hearkeneth unto counsel is wise.

A fool's wrath is presently known:
    but a prudent man covereth shame.

He that speaketh truth sheweth forth righteousness:
    but a false witness deceit.

There is that speaketh like the piercings of a sword:
    but the tongue of the wise is health.

The lip of truth shall be established for ever:
    but a lying tongue is but for a moment.

Deceit is in the heart of them that imagine evil:
    but to the counsellors of peace is joy.

There shall no evil happen to the just:
    but the wicked shall be filled with mischief.

Lying lips are abomination to the Lord:
    but they that deal truly are his delight.

A prudent man concealeth knowledge:
    but the heart of fools proclaimeth foolishness.

The hand of the diligent shall bear rule:
    but the slothful shall be under tribute.

Heaviness in the heart of man maketh it stoop:
    but a good word maketh it glad.

The righteous is more excellent than his neighbour:
    but the way of the wicked seduceth them.

The slothful man roasteth not that which he took in hunting:
    but the substance of a diligent man is precious.

In the way of righteousness is life;
    and in the pathway thereof there is no death.

A wise son heareth his father's instruction:
    but a scorner heareth not rebuke.

A man shall eat good by the fruit of his mouth:
    but the soul of the transgressors shall eat violence.

He that keepeth his mouth keepeth his life:
    but he that openeth wide his lips shall have destruction.

The soul of the sluggard desireth, and hath nothing:
    but the soul of the diligent shall be made fat.

A righteous man hateth lying:
    but a wicked man is loathsome, and cometh to shame.

Righteousness keepeth him that is upright in the way:
    but wickedness overthroweth the sinner.

There is that maketh himself rich, yet hath nothing:
    there is that maketh himself poor, yet hath great riches.

The ransom of a man's life are his riches:
    but the poor heareth not rebuke.

The light of the righteous rejoiceth:
    but the lamp of the wicked shall be put out.

Only by pride cometh contention:
    but with the well advised is wisdom.

Wealth gotten by vanity shall be diminished:
    but he that gathereth by labour shall increase.

Hope deferred maketh the heart sick:
    but when the desire cometh, it is a tree of life.

Whoso despiseth the word shall be destroyed:
  but he that feareth the commandment shall be rewarded.

The law of the wise is a fountain of life,
  to depart from the snares of death.

Good understanding giveth favour:
  but the way of transgressors is hard.

Every prudent man dealeth with knowledge:
  but a fool layeth open his folly.

A wicked messenger falleth into mischief:
  but a faithful ambassador is health.

Poverty and shame shall be to him that refuseth instruction:
  but he that regardeth reproof shall be honoured.

The desire accomplished is sweet to the soul:
  but it is abomination to fools to depart from evil.

He that walketh with wise men shall be wise:
  but a companion of fools shall be destroyed.

Evil pursueth sinners:
  but to the righteous good shall be repayed.

A good man leaveth an inheritance to his children's children:
  and the wealth of the sinner is laid up for the just.

Much food is in the tillage of the poor:
  but there is that is destroyed for want of judgment.

He that spareth his rod hateth his son:
  but he that loveth him chasteneth him betimes.

The righteous eateth to the satisfying of his soul:
  but the belly of the wicked shall want.

Every wise woman buildeth her house:
  but the foolish plucketh it down with her hands.

He that walketh in his uprightness feareth the Lord:
  but he that is perverse in his ways despiseth him.

In the mouth of the foolish is a rod of pride:
  but the lips of the wise shall preserve them.

Where no oxen are, the crib is clean:
  but much increase is by the strength of the ox.

A faithful witness will not lie:
  but a false witness will utter lies.

A scorner seeketh wisdom, and findeth it not:
  but knowledge is easy unto him that understandeth.

Go from the presence of a foolish man,
  when thou perceivest not in him the lips of knowledge.

The wisdom of the prudent is to understand his way:
  but the folly of fools is deceit.

Fools make a mock at sin:
  but among the righteous there is favour.

The heart knoweth his own bitterness;
  and a stranger doth not intermeddle with his joy.

The house of the wicked shall be overthrown:
  but the tabernacle of the upright shall flourish.

There is a way which seemeth right unto a man,
  but the end thereof are the ways of death.

Even in laughter the heart is sorrowful;
  and the end of that mirth is heaviness.

The backslider in heart shall be filled with his own ways:
  and a good man shall be satisfied from himself.

The simple believeth every word:
  but the prudent man looketh well to his going.

A wise man feareth, and departeth from evil:
  but the fool rageth, and is confident.

He that is soon angry dealeth foolishly:
  and a man of wicked devices is hated.

The simple inherit folly:
  but the prudent are crowned with knowledge.

The evil bow before the good;
  and the wicked at the gates of the righteous.

The poor is hated even of his own neighbour:
  but the rich hath many friends.

He that despiseth his neighbour sinneth:
  but he that hath mercy on the poor, happy is he.

Do they not err that devise evil?
  but mercy and truth shall be to them that devise good.

In all labour there is profit:
  but the talk of the lips tendeth only to penury.

The crown of the wise is their riches:
  but the foolishness of fools is folly.

A true witness delivereth souls:
  but a deceitful witness speaketh lies.

In the fear of the Lord is strong confidence:
  and his children shall have a place of refuge.

The fear of the Lord is a fountain of life,
  to depart from the snares of death.

In the multitude of people is the king's honour:
  but in the want of people is the destruction of the prince.

He that is slow to wrath is of great understanding:
  but he that is hasty of spirit exalteth folly.

A sound heart is the life of the flesh:
  but envy the rottenness of the bones.

He that oppresseth the poor reproacheth his Maker:
  but he that honoureth him hath mercy on the poor.

The wicked is driven away in his wickedness:
  but the righteous hath hope in his death.

Wisdom resteth in the heart of him that hath understanding:
  but that which is in the midst of fools is made known.

Righteousness exalteth a nation:
  but sin is a reproach to any people.

The king's favour is toward a wise servant:
  but his wrath is against him that causeth shame.

A soft answer turneth away wrath:
  but grievous words stir up anger.

The tongue of the wise useth knowledge aright:
  but the mouth of fools poureth out foolishness.

The eyes of the Lord are in every place,
  beholding the evil and the good.

A wholesome tongue is a tree of life:
  but perverseness therein is a breach in the spirit.

A fool despiseth his father's instruction:
  but he that regardeth reproof is prudent.

In the house of the righteous is much treasure:
  but in the revenues of the wicked is trouble.

The lips of the wise disperse knowledge:
  but the heart of the foolish doeth not so.

The sacrifice of the wicked is an abomination to the Lord:
  but the prayer of the upright is his delight.

The way of the wicked is an abomination unto the Lord:
  but he loveth him that followeth after righteousness.

Correction is grievous unto him that forsaketh the way:
  and he that hateth reproof shall die.

Hell and destruction are before the Lord:
  how much more then the hearts of the children of men?

A scorner loveth not one that reproveth him:
  neither will he go unto the wise.

A merry heart maketh a cheerful countenance:
  but by sorrow of the heart the spirit is broken.

The heart of him that hath understanding seeketh knowledge:
  but the mouth of fools feedeth on foolishness.

All the days of the afflicted are evil:
  but he that is of a merry heart hath a continual feast.

Better is little with the fear of the Lord
  than great treasure and trouble therewith.

Better is a dinner of herbs where love is,
  than a stalled ox and hatred therewith.

A wrathful man stirreth up strife:
  but he that is slow to anger appeaseth strife.

The way of the slothful man is as an hedge of thorns:
  but the way of the righteous is made plain.

A wise son maketh a glad father:
  but a foolish man despiseth his mother.

Folly is joy to him that is destitute of wisdom:
  but a man of understanding walketh uprightly.

Without counsel purposes are disappointed:
  but in the multitude of counsellors they are established.

A man hath joy by the answer of his mouth:
  and a word spoken in due season, how good is it!

The way of life is above to the wise,
  that he may depart from hell beneath.

The Lord will destroy the house of the proud:
  but he will establish the border of the widow.

The thoughts of the wicked are an abomination to the Lord:
  but the words of the pure are pleasant words.

He that is greedy of gain troubleth his own house;
  but he that hateth gifts shall live.

The heart of the righteous studieth to answer:
    but the mouth of the wicked poureth out evil things.

The Lord is far from the wicked:
    but he heareth the prayer of the righteous.

The light of the eyes rejoiceth the heart:
    and a good report maketh the bones fat.

The ear that heareth the reproof of life
    abideth among the wise.

He that refuseth instruction despiseth his own soul:
    but he that heareth reproof getteth understanding.

The fear of the Lord is the instruction of wisdom;
    and before honour is humility.

The preparations of the heart in man,
    and the answer of the tongue, is from the Lord.

All the ways of a man are clean in his own eyes;
    but the Lord weigheth the spirits.

Commit thy works unto the Lord,
    and thy thoughts shall be established.

The Lord hath made all things for himself:
    yea, even the wicked for the day of evil.

Every one that is proud in heart is an abomination to the Lord:
    though hand join in hand, he shall not be unpunished.

By mercy and truth iniquity is purged:
    and by the fear of the Lord men depart from evil.

When a man's ways please the Lord,
    he maketh even his enemies to be at peace with him.

Better is a little with righteousness
    than great revenues without right.

A man's heart deviseth his way:
    but the Lord directeth his steps.

A divine sentence is in the lips of the king:
    his mouth transgresseth not in judgment.

A just weight and balance are the Lord's:
    all the weights of the bag are his work.

It is an abomination to kings to commit wickedness:
    for the throne is established by righteousness.

Righteous lips are the delight of kings;
    and they love him that speaketh right.

The wrath of a king is as messengers of death:
    but a wise man will pacify it.

In the light of the king's countenance is life;
    and his favour is as a cloud of the latter rain.

How much better is it to get wisdom than gold!
    and to get understanding rather to be chosen than silver!

The highway of the upright is to depart from evil:
    he that keepeth his way preserveth his soul.

Pride goeth before destruction,
    and an haughty spirit before a fall.

Better it is to be of an humble spirit with the lowly,
    than to divide the spoil with the proud.

He that handleth a matter wisely shall find good:
    and whoso trusteth in the Lord, happy is he.

The wise in heart shall be called prudent:
    and the sweetness of the lips increaseth learning.

Understanding is a wellspring of life unto him that hath it:
    but the instruction of fools is folly.

The heart of the wise teacheth his mouth,
    and addeth learning to his lips.

Pleasant words are as an honeycomb,
    sweet to the soul, and health to the bones.

There is a way that seemeth right unto a man,
    but the end thereof are the ways of death.

He that laboureth laboureth for himself;
    for his mouth craveth it of him.

An ungodly man diggeth up evil:
    and in his lips there is as a burning fire.

A froward man soweth strife:
    and a whisperer separateth chief friends.

A violent man enticeth his neighbour,
    and leadeth him into the way that is not good.

He shutteth his eyes to devise froward things:
    moving his lips he bringeth evil to pass.

The hoary head is a crown of glory,
    if it be found in the way of righteousness.

He that is slow to anger is better than the mighty;
    and he that ruleth his spirit than he that taketh a city.

The lot is cast into the lap;
    but the whole disposing thereof is of the Lord.

Better is a dry morsel, and quietness therewith,
    than an house full of sacrifices with strife.

A wise servant shall have rule over a son that causeth shame,
    and shall have part of the inheritance among the brethren.

The fining pot is for silver, and the furnace for gold:
    but the Lord trieth the hearts.

A wicked doer giveth heed to false lips;
    and a liar giveth ear to a naughty tongue.

Whoso mocketh the poor reproacheth his Maker:
    and he that is glad at calamities shall not be unpunished.

Children's children are the crown of old men;
    and the glory of children are their fathers.

Excellent speech becometh not a fool:
much less do lying lips a prince.

A gift is as a precious stone in the eyes of him that hath it:
whithersoever it turneth, it prospereth.

He that covereth a transgression seeketh love;
but he that repeateth a matter separateth very friends.

A reproof entereth more into a wise man
than an hundred stripes into a fool.

An evil man seeketh only rebellion:
therefore a cruel messenger shall be sent against him.

Let a bear robbed of her whelps meet a man,
rather than a fool in his folly.

Whoso rewardeth evil for good,
evil shall not depart from his house.

The beginning of strife is as when one letteth out water:
therefore leave off contention, before it be meddled with.

He that justifieth the wicked, and he that condemneth the just,
even they both are abomination to the Lord.

Wherefore is there a price in the hand of a fool to get wisdom,
seeing he hath no heart to it?

A friend loveth at all times,
and a brother is born for adversity.

A man void of understanding striketh hands,
and becometh surety in the presence of his friend.

He loveth transgression that loveth strife:
and he that exalteth his gate seeketh destruction.

He that hath a froward heart findeth no good:
and he that hath a perverse tongue falleth into mischief.

He that begetteth a fool doeth it to his sorrow:
and the father of a fool hath no joy.

A merry heart doeth good like a medicine:
  but a broken spirit drieth the bones.

A wicked man taketh a gift out of the bosom
  to pervert the ways of judgment.

Wisdom is before him that hath understanding;
  but the eyes of a fool are in the ends of the earth.

A foolish son is a grief to his father,
  and bitterness to her that bare him.

Also to punish the just is not good,
  nor to strike princes for equity.

He that hath knowledge spareth his words:
  and a man of understanding is of an excellent spirit.

Even a fool, when he holdeth his peace, is counted wise:
  and he that shutteth his lips is esteemed a man of understanding.

Through desire a man, having separated himself,
  seeketh and intermeddleth with all wisdom.

A fool hath no delight in understanding,
  but that his heart may discover itself.

When the wicked cometh, then cometh also contempt,
  and with ignominy reproach.

The words of a man's mouth are as deep waters,
  and the wellspring of wisdom as a flowing brook.

It is not good to accept the person of the wicked,
  to overthrow the righteous in judgment.

A fool's lips enter into contention,
  and his mouth calleth for strokes.

A fool's mouth is his destruction,
  and his lips are the snare of his soul.

The words of a talebearer are as wounds,
  and they go down into the innermost parts of the belly.

He also that is slothful in his work
  is brother to him that is a great waster.

The name of the Lord is a strong tower:
  the righteous runneth into it, and is safe.

The rich man's wealth is his strong city,
  and as an high wall in his own conceit.

Before destruction the heart of man is haughty,
  and before honour is humility.

He that answereth a matter before he heareth it,
  it is folly and shame unto him.

The spirit of a man will sustain his infirmity;
  but a wounded spirit who can bear?

The heart of the prudent getteth knowledge;
  and the ear of the wise seeketh knowledge.

A man's gift maketh room for him,
  and bringeth him before great men.

He that is first in his own cause seemeth just;
  but his neighbour cometh and searcheth him.

The lot causeth contentions to cease,
  and parteth between the mighty.

A brother offended is harder to be won than a strong city:
  and their contentions are like the bars of a castle.

A man's belly shall be satisfied with the fruit of his mouth;
  and with the increase of his lips shall he be filled.

Death and life are in the power of the tongue:
  and they that love it shall eat the fruit thereof.

Whoso findeth a wife findeth a good thing,
  and obtaineth favour of the Lord.

The poor useth intreaties;
  but the rich answereth roughly.

A man that hath friends must shew himself friendly:
  and there is a friend that sticketh closer than a brother.

Better is the poor that walketh in his integrity,
  than he that is perverse in his lips, and is a fool.

Also, that the soul be without knowledge, it is not good;
  and he that hasteth with his feet sinneth.

The foolishness of man perverteth his way:
  and his heart fretteth against the Lord.

Wealth maketh many friends;
  but the poor is separated from his neighbour.

A false witness shall not be unpunished,
  and he that speaketh lies shall not escape.

Many will intreat the favour of the prince:
  and every man is a friend to him that giveth gifts.

All the brethren of the poor do hate him:
  how much more do his friends go far from him?
he pursueth them with words,
  yet they are wanting to him.

He that getteth wisdom loveth his own soul:
  he that keepeth understanding shall find good.

A false witness shall not be unpunished,
  and he that speaketh lies shall perish.

Delight is not seemly for a fool;
  much less for a servant to have rule over princes.

The discretion of a man deferreth his anger;
  and it is his glory to pass over a transgression.

The king's wrath is as the roaring of a lion;
  but his favour is as dew upon the grass.

A foolish son is the calamity of his father:
  and the contentions of a wife are a continual dropping.

House and riches are the inheritance of fathers:
    and a prudent wife is from the Lord.

Slothfulness casteth into a deep sleep;
    and an idle soul shall suffer hunger.

He that keepeth the commandment keepeth his own soul;
    but he that despiseth his ways shall die.

He that hath pity upon the poor lendeth unto the Lord;
    and that which he hath given will he pay him again.

Chasten thy son while there is hope,
    and let not thy soul spare for his crying.

A man of great wrath shall suffer punishment:
    for if thou deliver him, yet thou must do it again.

Hear counsel, and receive instruction,
    that thou mayest be wise in thy latter end.

There are many devices in a man's heart;
    nevertheless the counsel of the Lord, that shall stand.

The desire of a man is his kindness:
    and a poor man is better than a liar.

The fear of the Lord tendeth to life:
    and he that hath it shall abide satisfied;
    he shall not be visited with evil.

A slothful man hideth his hand in his bosom,
    and will not so much as bring it to his mouth again.

Smite a scorner,
    and the simple will beware:
and reprove one that hath understanding,
    and he will understand knowledge.

He that wasteth his father, and chaseth away his mother,
    is a son that causeth shame, and bringeth reproach.

Cease, my son, to hear the instruction
    that causeth to err from the words of knowledge.

An ungodly witness scorneth judgment:
    and the mouth of the wicked devoureth iniquity.

Judgments are prepared for scorners,
    and stripes for the back of fools.

Wine is a mocker, strong drink is raging:
    and whosoever is deceived thereby is not wise.

The fear of a king is as the roaring of a lion:
    whoso provoketh him to anger sinneth against his own soul.

It is an honour for a man to cease from strife:
    but every fool will be meddling.

The sluggard will not plow by reason of the cold;
    therefore shall he beg in harvest, and have nothing.

Counsel in the heart of man is like deep water;
    but a man of understanding will draw it out.

Most men will proclaim every one his own goodness:
    but a faithful man who can find?

The just man walketh in his integrity:
    his children are blessed after him.

A king that sitteth in the throne of judgment
    scattereth away all evil with his eyes.

Who can say, I have made my heart clean,
    I am pure from my sin?

Divers weights, and divers measures,
    both of them are alike abomination to the Lord.

Even a child is known by his doings,
    whether his work be pure, and whether it be right.

The hearing ear, and the seeing eye,
    the Lord hath made even both of them.

Love not sleep, lest thou come to poverty;
    open thine eyes, and thou shalt be satisfied with bread.

It is naught, it is naught, saith the buyer:
    but when he is gone his way, then he boasteth.

There is gold, and a multitude of rubies:
    but the lips of knowledge are a precious jewel.

Take his garment that is surety for a stranger:
    and take a pledge of him for a strange woman.

Bread of deceit is sweet to a man;
    but afterwards his mouth shall be filled with gravel.

Every purpose is established by counsel:
    and with good advice make war.

He that goeth about as a talebearer revealeth secrets:
    therefore meddle not with him that flattereth with his lips.

Whoso curseth his father or his mother,
    his lamp shall be put out in obscure darkness.

An inheritance may be gotten hastily at the beginning;
    but the end thereof shall not be blessed.

Say not thou, I will recompense evil;
    but wait on the Lord, and he shall save thee.

Divers weights are an abomination unto the Lord;
    and a false balance is not good.

Man's goings are of the Lord;
    how can a man then understand his own way?

It is a snare to the man who devoureth that which is holy,
    and after vows to make inquiry.

A wise king scattereth the wicked,
    and bringeth the wheel over them.

The spirit of man is the candle of the Lord,
    searching all the inward parts of the belly.

Mercy and truth preserve the king:
    and his throne is upholden by mercy.

The glory of young men is their strength:
    and the beauty of old men is the gray head.

The blueness of a wound cleanseth away evil:
    so do stripes the inward parts of the belly.

The king's heart is in the hand of the Lord, as the rivers of water:
    he turneth it whithersoever he will.

Every way of a man is right in his own eyes:
    but the Lord pondereth the hearts.

To do justice and judgment
    is more acceptable to the Lord than sacrifice.

An high look, and a proud heart,
    and the plowing of the wicked, is sin.

The thoughts of the diligent tend only to plenteousness;
    but of every one that is hasty only to want.

The getting of treasures by a lying tongue
    is a vanity tossed to and fro of them that seek death.

The robbery of the wicked shall destroy them;
    because they refuse to do judgment.

The way of man is froward and strange:
    but as for the pure, his work is right.

It is better to dwell in a corner of the housetop,
    than with a brawling woman in a wide house.

The soul of the wicked desireth evil:
    his neighbour findeth no favour in his eyes.

When the scorner is punished, the simple is made wise:
    and when the wise is instructed, he receiveth knowledge.

The righteous man wisely considereth the house of the wicked:
    but God overthroweth the wicked for their wickedness.

Whoso stoppeth his ears at the cry of the poor,
    he also shall cry himself, but shall not be heard.

A gift in secret pacifieth anger:
  and a reward in the bosom strong wrath.

It is joy to the just to do judgment:
  but destruction shall be to the workers of iniquity.

The man that wandereth out of the way of understanding
  shall remain in the congregation of the dead.

He that loveth pleasure shall be a poor man:
  he that loveth wine and oil shall not be rich.

The wicked shall be a ransom for the righteous,
  and the transgressor for the upright.

It is better to dwell in the wilderness,
  than with a contentious and an angry woman.

There is treasure to be desired and oil in the dwelling of the wise;
  but a foolish man spendeth it up.

He that followeth after righteousness and mercy
  findeth life, righteousness, and honour.

A wise man scaleth the city of the mighty,
  and casteth down the strength of the confidence thereof.

Whoso keepeth his mouth and his tongue
  keepeth his soul from troubles.

Proud and haughty scorner is his name,
  who dealeth in proud wrath.

The desire of the slothful killeth him;
  for his hands refuse to labour.

He coveteth greedily all the day long:
  but the righteous giveth and spareth not.

The sacrifice of the wicked is abomination:
  how much more, when he bringeth it with a wicked mind?

A false witness shall perish:
  but the man that heareth speaketh constantly.

A wicked man hardeneth his face:
    but as for the upright, he directeth his way.

There is no wisdom nor understanding nor counsel
    against the Lord.

The horse is prepared against the day of battle:
    but safety is of the Lord.

A good name is rather to be chosen than great riches,
    and loving favour rather than silver and gold.

The rich and poor meet together:
    the Lord is the maker of them all.

A prudent man foreseeth the evil, and hideth himself:
    but the simple pass on, and are punished.

By humility and the fear of the Lord
    are riches, and honour, and life.

Thorns and snares are in the way of the froward:
    he that doth keep his soul shall be far from them.

Train up a child in the way he should go:
    and when he is old, he will not depart from it.

The rich ruleth over the poor,
    and the borrower is servant to the lender.

He that soweth iniquity shall reap vanity:
    and the rod of his anger shall fail.

He that hath a bountiful eye shall be blessed;
    for he giveth of his bread to the poor.

Cast out the scorner, and contention shall go out;
    yea, strife and reproach shall cease.

He that loveth pureness of heart,
    for the grace of his lips the king shall be his friend.

The eyes of the Lord preserve knowledge,
    and he overthroweth the words of the transgressor.

The slothful man saith,
There is a lion without, I shall be slain in the streets.

The mouth of strange women is a deep pit:
he that is abhorred of the Lord shall fall therein.

Foolishness is bound in the heart of a child;
but the rod of correction shall drive it far from him.

He that oppresseth the poor to increase his riches,
and he that giveth to the rich,
shall surely come to want.

WORDS OF THE WISE
Proverbs 22:17 – 24:22

Bow down thine ear, and hear the words of the wise,
and apply thine heart unto my knowledge.
For it is a pleasant thing if thou keep them within thee;
they shall withal be fitted in thy lips.
That thy trust may be in the Lord,
I have made known to thee this day, even to thee.
Have not I written to thee excellent things
in counsels and knowledge,
That I might make thee know the certainty
of the words of truth;
that thou mightest answer the words of truth
to them that send unto thee?

Rob not the poor, because he is poor:
neither oppress the afflicted in the gate:
For the Lord will plead their cause,
and spoil the soul of those that spoiled them.

Make no friendship with an angry man;
and with a furious man thou shalt not go:
Lest thou learn his ways, and get a snare to thy soul.

Be not thou one of them that strike hands,
or of them that are sureties for debts.

If thou hast nothing to pay,
    why should he take away thy bed from under thee?

Remove not the ancient landmark,
    which thy fathers have set.

Seest thou a man diligent in his business?
    he shall stand before kings;
    he shall not stand before mean men.

When thou sittest to eat with a ruler,
    consider diligently what is before thee:
And put a knife to thy throat,
    if thou be a man given to appetite.
Be not desirous of his dainties:
    for they are deceitful meat.

Labour not to be rich:
    cease from thine own wisdom.
Wilt thou set thine eyes upon that which is not?
    for riches certainly make themselves wings;
    they fly away as an eagle toward heaven.

Eat thou not the bread of him that hath an evil eye,
    neither desire thou his dainty meats:
For as he thinketh in his heart, so is he:
Eat and drink, saith he to thee;
    but his heart is not with thee.
The morsel which thou hast eaten shalt thou vomit up,
    and lose thy sweet words.

Speak not in the ears of a fool:
    for he will despise the wisdom of thy words.

Remove not the old landmark;
    and enter not into the fields of the fatherless:
For their redeemer is mighty;
    he shall plead their cause with thee.

Apply thine heart unto instruction,
    and thine ears to the words of knowledge.

Withhold not correction from the child:
    for if thou beatest him with the rod, he shall not die.
Thou shalt beat him with the rod,
    and shalt deliver his soul from hell.

My son, if thine heart be wise,
    my heart shall rejoice, even mine.
Yea, my reins shall rejoice,
    when thy lips speak right things.

Let not thine heart envy sinners:
    but be thou in the fear of the Lord all the day long.
For surely there is an end;
    and thine expectation shall not be cut off.

Hear thou, my son, and be wise,
    and guide thine heart in the way.
Be not among winebibbers;
    among riotous eaters of flesh:
For the drunkard and the glutton shall come to poverty:
    and drowsiness shall clothe a man with rags.

Hearken unto thy father that begat thee,
    and despise not thy mother when she is old.
Buy the truth, and sell it not;
    also wisdom, and instruction, and understanding.
The father of the righteous shall greatly rejoice:
    and he that begetteth a wise child shall have joy of him.
Thy father and thy mother shall be glad,
    and she that bare thee shall rejoice.

My son, give me thine heart,
    and let thine eyes observe my ways.
For a whore is a deep ditch;
    and a strange woman is a narrow pit.
She also lieth in wait as for a prey,
    and increaseth the transgressors among men.

Who hath woe? who hath sorrow? who hath contentions?
    who hath babbling? who hath wounds without cause?
    who hath redness of eyes?

71

They that tarry long at the wine;
    they that go to seek mixed wine.

Look not thou upon the wine when it is red,
    when it giveth his colour in the cup,
    when it moveth itself aright.
At the last it biteth like a serpent,
    and stingeth like an adder.
Thine eyes shall behold strange women,
    and thine heart shall utter perverse things.
Yea, thou shalt be
    as he that lieth down in the midst of the sea,
    or as he that lieth upon the top of a mast.
They have stricken me, shalt thou say,
    and I was not sick;
they have beaten me,
    and I felt it not:
when shall I awake?
    I will seek it yet again.

Be not thou envious against evil men,
    neither desire to be with them.
For their heart studieth destruction,
    and their lips talk of mischief.

Through wisdom is an house builded;
    and by understanding it is established:
And by knowledge shall the chambers be filled
    with all precious and pleasant riches.

A wise man is strong;
    yea, a man of knowledge increaseth strength.
For by wise counsel thou shalt make thy war:
    and in multitude of counsellors there is safety.

Wisdom is too high for a fool:
    he openeth not his mouth in the gate.

He that deviseth to do evil
    shall be called a mischievous person.

The thought of foolishness is sin:
  and the scorner is an abomination to men.

If thou faint in the day of adversity,
  thy strength is small.

If thou forbear to deliver them that are drawn unto death,
  and those that are ready to be slain;
If thou sayest, Behold, we knew it not;
  doth not he that pondereth the heart consider it?
and he that keepeth thy soul, doth not he know it?
  and shall not he render to every man
  according to his works?

My son, eat thou honey, because it is good;
  and the honeycomb, which is sweet to thy taste:
So shall the knowledge of wisdom be unto thy soul:
  when thou hast found it, then there shall be a reward,
  and thy expectation shall not be cut off.

Lay not wait, O wicked man,
  against the dwelling of the righteous;
  spoil not his resting place:
For a just man falleth seven times, and riseth up again:
  but the wicked shall fall into mischief.

Rejoice not when thine enemy falleth,
  and let not thine heart be glad when he stumbleth:
Lest the Lord see it, and it displease him,
  and he turn away his wrath from him.

Fret not thyself because of evil men,
  neither be thou envious at the wicked;
For there shall be no reward to the evil man;
  the candle of the wicked shall be put out.

My son, fear thou the Lord and the king:
  and meddle not with them that are given to change:
For their calamity shall rise suddenly;
  and who knoweth the ruin of them both?

MORE WORDS OF THE WISE
Proverbs 24:23–34

These things also belong to the wise.

It is not good to have respect of persons in judgment.
He that saith unto the wicked, Thou art righteous;
    him shall the people curse, nations shall abhor him:
But to them that rebuke him shall be delight,
    and a good blessing shall come upon them.

Every man shall kiss his lips
    that giveth a right answer.

Prepare thy work without, and make it fit for thyself in the field;
    and afterwards build thine house.

Be not a witness against thy neighbour without cause;
    and deceive not with thy lips.
Say not, I will do so to him as he hath done to me:
    I will render to the man according to his work.

I went by the field of the slothful,
    and by the vineyard of the man void of understanding;
And, lo, it was all grown over with thorns,
    and nettles had covered the face thereof,
    and the stone wall thereof was broken down.
Then I saw, and considered it well:
    I looked upon it, and received instruction.
Yet a little sleep, a little slumber,
    a little folding of the hands to sleep:
So shall thy poverty come as one that travelleth;
    and thy want as an armed man.

MORE PROVERBS OF SOLOMON
Proverbs 25:1 – 29:27

These are also proverbs of Solomon, which the men of Hezekiah king
of Judah copied out.

It is the glory of God to conceal a thing:
  but the honour of kings is to search out a matter.

The heaven for height, and the earth for depth,
  and the heart of kings is unsearchable.

Take away the dross from the silver,
  and there shall come forth a vessel for the finer.
Take away the wicked from before the king,
  and his throne shall be established in righteousness.

Put not forth thyself in the presence of the king,
  and stand not in the place of great men:
For better it is that it be said unto thee, Come up hither;
  than that thou shouldest be put lower
  in the presence of the prince whom thine eyes have seen.

Go not forth hastily to strive,
  lest thou know not what to do in the end thereof,
  when thy neighbour hath put thee to shame.

Debate thy cause with thy neighbour himself;
  and discover not a secret to another:
Lest he that heareth it put thee to shame,
  and thine infamy turn not away.

A word fitly spoken is like apples of gold in pictures of silver.

As an earring of gold, and an ornament of fine gold,
  so is a wise reprover upon an obedient ear.

As the cold of snow in the time of harvest,
  so is a faithful messenger to them that send him:
  for he refresheth the soul of his masters.

Whoso boasteth himself of a false gift
  is like clouds and wind without rain.

By long forbearing is a prince persuaded,
  and a soft tongue breaketh the bone.

Hast thou found honey? eat so much as is sufficient for thee,
  lest thou be filled therewith, and vomit it.

Withdraw thy foot from thy neighbour's house;
    lest he be weary of thee, and so hate thee.

A man that beareth false witness against his neighbour
    is a maul, and a sword, and a sharp arrow.

Confidence in an unfaithful man in time of trouble
    is like a broken tooth, and a foot out of joint.

As he that taketh away a garment in cold weather,
    and as vinegar upon nitre,
    so is he that singeth songs to an heavy heart.

If thine enemy be hungry, give him bread to eat;
    and if he be thirsty, give him water to drink:
For thou shalt heap coals of fire upon his head,
    and the Lord shall reward thee.

The north wind driveth away rain:
    so doth an angry countenance a backbiting tongue.

It is better to dwell in the corner of the housetop,
    than with a brawling woman and in a wide house.

As cold waters to a thirsty soul,
    so is good news from a far country.

A righteous man falling down before the wicked
    is as a troubled fountain, and a corrupt spring.

It is not good to eat much honey:
    so for men to search their own glory is not glory.

He that hath no rule over his own spirit
    is like a city that is broken down, and without walls.

As snow in summer, and as rain in harvest,
    so honour is not seemly for a fool.

As the bird by wandering, as the swallow by flying,
    so the curse causeless shall not come.

A whip for the horse, a bridle for the ass,
    and a rod for the fool's back.

Answer not a fool according to his folly,
　　lest thou also be like unto him.

Answer a fool according to his folly,
　　lest he be wise in his own conceit.

He that sendeth a message by the hand of a fool
　　cutteth off the feet, and drinketh damage.

The legs of the lame are not equal:
　　so is a parable in the mouth of fools.

As he that bindeth a stone in a sling,
　　so is he that giveth honour to a fool.

As a thorn goeth up into the hand of a drunkard,
　　so is a parable in the mouth of fools.

The great God that formed all things both rewardeth the fool,
　　and rewardeth transgressors.

As a dog returneth to his vomit,
　　so a fool returneth to his folly.

Seest thou a man wise in his own conceit?
　　there is more hope of a fool than of him.

The slothful man saith, There is a lion in the way;
　　a lion is in the streets.

As the door turneth upon his hinges,
　　so doth the slothful upon his bed.

The slothful hideth his hand in his bosom;
　　it grieveth him to bring it again to his mouth.

The sluggard is wiser in his own conceit
　　than seven men that can render a reason.

He that passeth by, and meddleth with strife belonging not to him,
　　is like one that taketh a dog by the ears.

As a mad man who casteth firebrands, arrows, and death,
So is the man that deceiveth his neighbour,
　　and saith, Am not I in sport?

Where no wood is, there the fire goeth out:
    so where there is no talebearer, the strife ceaseth.

As coals are to burning coals, and wood to fire;
    so is a contentious man to kindle strife.

The words of a talebearer are as wounds,
    and they go down into the innermost parts of the belly.

Burning lips and a wicked heart
    are like a potsherd covered with silver dross.

He that hateth dissembleth with his lips,
    and layeth up deceit within him;
When he speaketh fair, believe him not:
    for there are seven abominations in his heart.

Whose hatred is covered by deceit,
    his wickedness shall be shewed before the whole congregation.

Whoso diggeth a pit shall fall therein:
    and he that rolleth a stone, it will return upon him.

A lying tongue hateth those that are afflicted by it;
    and a flattering mouth worketh ruin.

Boast not thyself of to morrow;
    for thou knowest not what a day may bring forth.

Let another man praise thee, and not thine own mouth;
    a stranger, and not thine own lips.

A stone is heavy, and the sand weighty;
    but a fool's wrath is heavier than them both.

Wrath is cruel, and anger is outrageous;
    but who is able to stand before envy?

Open rebuke is better than secret love.

Faithful are the wounds of a friend;
    but the kisses of an enemy are deceitful.

The full soul loatheth an honeycomb;
    but to the hungry soul every bitter thing is sweet.

As a bird that wandereth from her nest,
　　so is a man that wandereth from his place.

Ointment and perfume rejoice the heart:
　　so doth the sweetness of a man's friend by hearty counsel.

Thine own friend, and thy father's friend, forsake not;
　　neither go into thy brother's house in the day of thy calamity:
　　for better is a neighbour that is near than a brother far off.

My son, be wise, and make my heart glad,
　　that I may answer him that reproacheth me.

A prudent man foreseeth the evil, and hideth himself;
　　but the simple pass on, and are punished.

Take his garment that is surety for a stranger,
　　and take a pledge of him for a strange woman.

He that blesseth his friend with a loud voice,
　　rising early in the morning,
　　it shall be counted a curse to him.

A continual dropping in a very rainy day
　　and a contentious woman are alike.
Whosoever hideth her hideth the wind,
　　and the ointment of his right hand,
　　which bewrayeth itself.

Iron sharpeneth iron;
　　so a man sharpeneth the countenance of his friend.

Whoso keepeth the fig tree shall eat the fruit thereof:
　　so he that waiteth on his master shall be honoured.

As in water face answereth to face,
　　so the heart of man to man.

Hell and destruction are never full;
　　so the eyes of man are never satisfied.

As the fining pot for silver, and the furnace for gold;
　　so is a man to his praise.

Though thou shouldest bray a fool in a mortar
    among wheat with a pestle,
       yet will not his foolishness depart from him.

Be thou diligent to know the state of thy flocks,
    and look well to thy herds.
For riches are not for ever:
    and doth the crown endure to every generation?
The hay appeareth, and the tender grass sheweth itself,
    and herbs of the mountains are gathered.
The lambs are for thy clothing,
    and the goats are the price of the field.
And thou shalt have goats' milk enough for thy food,
    for the food of thy household,
       and for the maintenance for thy maidens.

The wicked flee when no man pursueth:
    but the righteous are bold as a lion.

For the transgression of a land many are the princes thereof:
    but by a man of understanding and knowledge
    the state thereof shall be prolonged.

A poor man that oppresseth the poor
    is like a sweeping rain which leaveth no food.

They that forsake the law praise the wicked:
    but such as keep the law contend with them.

Evil men understand not judgment:
    but they that seek the Lord understand all things.

Better is the poor that walketh in his uprightness,
    than he that is perverse in his ways, though he be rich.

Whoso keepeth the law is a wise son:
    but he that is a companion of riotous men shameth his father.

He that by usury and unjust gain increaseth his substance,
    he shall gather it for him that will pity the poor.

He that turneth away his ear from hearing the law,
    even his prayer shall be abomination.

Whoso causeth the righteous to go astray in an evil way,
he shall fall himself into his own pit:
but the upright shall have good things in possession.

The rich man is wise in his own conceit;
but the poor that hath understanding searcheth him out.

When righteous men do rejoice, there is great glory:
but when the wicked rise, a man is hidden.

He that covereth his sins shall not prosper:
but whoso confesseth and forsaketh them shall have mercy.

Happy is the man that feareth alway:
but he that hardeneth his heart shall fall into mischief.

As a roaring lion, and a ranging bear;
so is a wicked ruler over the poor people.

The prince that wanteth understanding is also a great oppressor:
but he that hateth covetousness shall prolong his days.

A man that doeth violence to the blood of any person
shall flee to the pit; let no man stay him.

Whoso walketh uprightly shall be saved:
but he that is perverse in his ways shall fall at once.

He that tilleth his land shall have plenty of bread:
but he that followeth after vain persons
shall have poverty enough.

A faithful man shall abound with blessings:
but he that maketh haste to be rich shall not be innocent.

To have respect of persons is not good:
for for a piece of bread that man will transgress.

He that hasteth to be rich hath an evil eye,
and considereth not that poverty shall come upon him.

He that rebuketh a man afterwards shall find more favour
than he that flattereth with the tongue.

Whoso robbeth his father or his mother, and saith,
    It is no transgression;
    the same is the companion of a destroyer.

He that is of a proud heart stirreth up strife:
    but he that putteth his trust in the Lord shall be made fat.

He that trusteth in his own heart is a fool:
    but whoso walketh wisely, he shall be delivered.

He that giveth unto the poor shall not lack:
    but he that hideth his eyes shall have many a curse.

When the wicked rise, men hide themselves:
    but when they perish, the righteous increase.

He, that being often reproved hardeneth his neck,
    shall suddenly be destroyed, and that without remedy.

When the righteous are in authority, the people rejoice:
    but when the wicked beareth rule, the people mourn.

Whoso loveth wisdom rejoiceth his father:
    but he that keepeth company with harlots spendeth his substance.

The king by judgment establisheth the land:
    but he that receiveth gifts overthroweth it.

A man that flattereth his neighbour
    spreadeth a net for his feet.

In the transgression of an evil man there is a snare:
    but the righteous doth sing and rejoice.

The righteous considereth the cause of the poor:
    but the wicked regardeth not to know it.

Scornful men bring a city into a snare:
    but wise men turn away wrath.

If a wise man contendeth with a foolish man,
    whether he rage or laugh, there is no rest.

The bloodthirsty hate the upright:
    but the just seek his soul.

A fool uttereth all his mind:
　　but a wise man keepeth it in till afterwards.

If a ruler hearken to lies,
　　all his servants are wicked.

The poor and the deceitful man meet together:
　　the Lord lighteneth both their eyes.

The king that faithfully judgeth the poor,
　　his throne shall be established for ever.

The rod and reproof give wisdom:
　　but a child left to himself bringeth his mother to shame.

When the wicked are multiplied, transgression increaseth:
　　but the righteous shall see their fall.

Correct thy son, and he shall give thee rest;
　　yea, he shall give delight unto thy soul.

Where there is no vision, the people perish:
　　but he that keepeth the law, happy is he.

A servant will not be corrected by words:
　　for though he understand he will not answer.

Seest thou a man that is hasty in his words?
　　there is more hope of a fool than of him.

He that delicately bringeth up his servant from a child
　　shall have him become his son at the length.

An angry man stirreth up strife,
　　and a furious man aboundeth in transgression.

A man's pride shall bring him low:
　　but honour shall uphold the humble in spirit.

Whoso is partner with a thief hateth his own soul:
　　he heareth cursing, and bewrayeth it not.

The fear of man bringeth a snare:
　　but whoso putteth his trust in the Lord shall be safe.

Many seek the ruler's favour;
    but every man's judgment cometh from the Lord.

An unjust man is an abomination to the just:
    and he that is upright in the way is abomination to the wicked.

WORDS OF AGUR
Proverbs 30:1–33

The words of Agur the son of Jakeh, even the prophecy: the man
spake unto Ithiel, even unto Ithiel and Ucal,

Surely I am more brutish than any man,
    and have not the understanding of a man.
I neither learned wisdom,
    nor have the knowledge of the holy.
Who hath ascended up into heaven, or descended?
    who hath gathered the wind in his fists?
    who hath bound the waters in a garment?
    who hath established all the ends of the earth?
    what is his name, and what is his son's name, if thou canst tell?

Every word of God is pure:
    he is a shield unto them that put their trust in him.
Add thou not unto his words,
    lest he reprove thee, and thou be found a liar.

Two things have I required of thee;
    deny me them not before I die:
Remove far from me vanity and lies:
    give me neither poverty nor riches;
    feed me with food convenient for me:
Lest I be full, and deny thee, and say, Who is the Lord?
    or lest I be poor, and steal, and take the name of my God in vain.

Accuse not a servant unto his master,
    lest he curse thee, and thou be found guilty.

There is a generation that curseth their father,
    and doth not bless their mother.

There is a generation that are pure in their own eyes,
    and yet is not washed from their filthiness.
There is a generation, O how lofty are their eyes!
    and their eyelids are lifted up.
There is a generation, whose teeth are as swords,
    and their jaw teeth as knives,
to devour the poor from off the earth,
    and the needy from among men.

The horseleach hath two daughters,
    crying, Give, give.

There are three things that are never satisfied,
    yea, four things say not, It is enough:
The grave; and the barren womb;
    the earth that is not filled with water;
    and the fire that saith not, It is enough.

The eye that mocketh at his father,
    and despiseth to obey his mother,
the ravens of the valley shall pick it out,
    and the young eagles shall eat it.

There be three things which are too wonderful for me,
    yea, four which I know not:
The way of an eagle in the air;
    the way of a serpent upon a rock;
    the way of a ship in the midst of the sea;
    and the way of a man with a maid.

Such is the way of an adulterous woman;
    she eateth, and wipeth her mouth, and saith,
    I have done no wickedness.

For three things the earth is disquieted,
    and for four which it cannot bear:
For a servant when he reigneth;
    and a fool when he is filled with meat;
For an odious woman when she is married;
    and an handmaid that is heir to her mistress.

There be four things which are little upon the earth,
    but they are exceeding wise:
The ants are a people not strong,
    yet they prepare their meat in the summer;
The conies are but a feeble folk,
    yet make they their houses in the rocks;
The locusts have no king,
    yet go they forth all of them by bands;
The spider taketh hold with her hands,
    and is in kings' palaces.

There be three things which go well,
    yea, four are comely in going:
A lion which is strongest among beasts,
    and turneth not away for any;
A greyhound; an he goat also;
    and a king, against whom there is no rising up.

If thou hast done foolishly in lifting up thyself,
    or if thou hast thought evil, lay thine hand upon thy mouth.
Surely the churning of milk bringeth forth butter,
    and the wringing of the nose bringeth forth blood:
    so the forcing of wrath bringeth forth strife.

WORDS OF LEMUEL
Proverbs 31:1–9

The words of king Lemuel, the prophecy that his mother taught him.

What, my son? and what, the son of my womb?
    and what, the son of my vows?
Give not thy strength unto women,
    nor thy ways to that which destroyeth kings.

It is not for kings, O Lemuel,
    it is not for kings to drink wine; nor for princes strong drink:
Lest they drink, and forget the law,
    and pervert the judgment of any of the afflicted.

Give strong drink unto him that is ready to perish,
　　and wine unto those that be of heavy hearts.
Let him drink, and forget his poverty,
　　and remember his misery no more.

Open thy mouth for the dumb in the cause of all
　　such as are appointed to destruction.
Open thy mouth, judge righteously,
　　and plead the cause of the poor and needy.

THE VIRTUOUS WOMAN
Proverbs 31:10–31

Who can find a virtuous woman?
　　for her price is far above rubies.
The heart of her husband doth safely trust in her,
　　so that he shall have no need of spoil.
She will do him good and not evil
　　all the days of her life.
She seeketh wool, and flax,
　　and worketh willingly with her hands.
She is like the merchants' ships;
　　she bringeth her food from afar.
She riseth also while it is yet night,
　　and giveth meat to her household,
　　and a portion to her maidens.
She considereth a field, and buyeth it:
　　with the fruit of her hands she planteth a vineyard.
She girdeth her loins with strength,
　　and strengtheneth her arms.
She perceiveth that her merchandise is good:
　　her candle goeth not out by night.
She layeth her hands to the spindle,
　　and her hands hold the distaff.
She stretcheth out her hand to the poor;
　　yea, she reacheth forth her hands to the needy.

She is not afraid of the snow for her household:
    for all her household are clothed with scarlet.
She maketh herself coverings of tapestry;
    her clothing is silk and purple.
Her husband is known in the gates,
    when he sitteth among the elders of the land.
She maketh fine linen, and selleth it;
    and delivereth girdles unto the merchant.
Strength and honour are her clothing;
    and she shall rejoice in time to come.
She openeth her mouth with wisdom;
    and in her tongue is the law of kindness.
She looketh well to the ways of her household,
    and eateth not the bread of idleness.
Her children arise up, and call her blessed;
    her husband also, and he praiseth her.
Many daughters have done virtuously,
    but thou excellest them all.
Favour is deceitful, and beauty is vain:
    but a woman that feareth the Lord, she shall be praised.
Give her of the fruit of her hands;
    and let her own works praise her in the gates.

Part Two

The Book of Ecclesiastes

THE VANITY OF LIFE
Ecclesiastes 1:1 – 2:26

The words of the Preacher, the son of David, king in Jerusalem.

Vanity of vanities, saith the Preacher, vanity of vanities;
    all is vanity.

What profit hath a man of all his labour
    which he taketh under the sun?
One generation passeth away,
    and another generation cometh:
    but the earth abideth for ever.
The sun also ariseth, and the sun goeth down,
    and hasteth to his place where he arose.
The wind goeth toward the south,
    and turneth about unto the north;
    it whirleth about continually,
    and the wind returneth again according to his circuits.
All the rivers run into the sea; yet the sea is not full;
    unto the place from whence the rivers come,
    thither they return again.
All things are full of labour; man cannot utter it:
    the eye is not satisfied with seeing,
    nor the ear filled with hearing.
The thing that hath been, it is that which shall be;
    and that which is done is that which shall be done:
    and there is no new thing under the sun.
Is there any thing whereof it may be said, See, this is new?
    it hath been already of old time, which was before us.

There is no remembrance of former things;
> neither shall there be any remembrance of things
> that are to come with those that shall come after.

I the Preacher was king over Israel in Jerusalem. And I gave my heart to seek and search out by wisdom concerning all things that are done under heaven: this sore travail hath God given to the sons of man to be exercised therewith. I have seen all the works that are done under the sun; and, behold, all is vanity and vexation of spirit.

That which is crooked cannot be made straight:
> and that which is wanting cannot be numbered.

I communed with mine own heart, saying, Lo, I am come to great estate, and have gotten more wisdom than all they that have been before me in Jerusalem: yea, my heart had great experience of wisdom and knowledge. And I gave my heart to know wisdom, and to know madness and folly: I perceived that this also is vexation of spirit.

For in much wisdom is much grief:
> and he that increaseth knowledge increaseth sorrow.

I said in mine heart, Go to now, I will prove thee with mirth, therefore enjoy pleasure: and, behold, this also is vanity. I said of laughter, It is mad: and of mirth, What doeth it? I sought in mine heart to give myself unto wine, yet acquainting mine heart with wisdom; and to lay hold on folly, till I might see what was that good for the sons of men, which they should do under the heaven all the days of their life.

I made me great works; I builded me houses; I planted me vineyards: I made me gardens and orchards, and I planted trees in them of all kind of fruits: I made me pools of water, to water therewith the wood that bringeth forth trees: I got me servants and maidens, and had servants born in my house; also I had great possessions of great and small cattle above all that were in Jerusalem before me: I gathered me also silver and gold, and the peculiar treasure of kings and of the provinces: I gat me men singers and women singers, and the delights of the sons of men, as musical instruments, and that of all sorts. So I was great, and increased more than all that were before me in Jerusalem: also my wisdom remained with me.

And whatsoever mine eyes desired I kept not from them,
I withheld not my heart from any joy;
>for my heart rejoiced in all my labour:
>and this was my portion of all my labour.
Then I looked on all the works that my hands had wrought,
>and on the labour that I had laboured to do:
>and, behold, all was vanity and vexation of spirit,
>and there was no profit under the sun.
And I turned myself to behold wisdom, and madness, and folly:
>for what can the man do that cometh after the king?
>even that which hath been already done.
Then I saw that wisdom excelleth folly,
>as far as light excelleth darkness.
The wise man's eyes are in his head;
>but the fool walketh in darkness:
>and I myself perceived also
>that one event happeneth to them all.

Then said I in my heart,

>As it happeneth to the fool, so it happeneth even to me;
>>and why was I then more wise?
>Then I said in my heart, that this also is vanity.
>For there is no remembrance of the wise more
>>than of the fool for ever;
>>seeing that which now is
>>in the days to come shall all be forgotten.
>And how dieth the wise man? as the fool.

Therefore I hated life; because the work that is wrought under the sun is grievous unto me: for all is vanity and vexation of spirit. Yea, I hated all my labour which I had taken under the sun: because I should leave it unto the man that shall be after me. And who knoweth whether he shall be a wise man or a fool? yet shall he have rule over all my labour wherein I have laboured, and wherein I have shewed myself wise under the sun. This is also vanity. Therefore I went about to cause my heart to despair of all the labour which I took under the sun. For there is a man whose labour is in wisdom, and in knowledge, and in equity;

yet to a man that hath not laboured therein shall he leave it for his portion. This also is vanity and a great evil. For what hath man of all his labour, and of the vexation of his heart, wherein he hath laboured under the sun? For all his days are sorrows, and his travail grief; yea, his heart taketh not rest in the night. This is also vanity.

There is nothing better for a man, than that he should eat and drink, and that he should make his soul enjoy good in his labour. This also I saw, that it was from the hand of God. For who can eat, or who else can hasten hereunto, more than I? For God giveth to a man that is good in his sight wisdom, and knowledge, and joy: but to the sinner he giveth travail, to gather and to heap up, that he may give to him that is good before God. This also is vanity and vexation of spirit.

TO EVERYTHING A SEASON
Ecclesiastes 3:1–22

To every thing there is a season, and a time to every purpose under the heaven:

> A time to be born, and a time to die;
>> a time to plant, and a time to pluck up that which is planted;
> A time to kill, and a time to heal;
>> a time to break down, and a time to build up;
> A time to weep, and a time to laugh;
>> a time to mourn, and a time to dance;
> A time to cast away stones, and a time to gather stones together;
>> a time to embrace, and a time to refrain from embracing;
> A time to get, and a time to lose;
>> a time to keep, and a time to cast away;
> A time to rend, and a time to sew;
>> a time to keep silence, and a time to speak;
> A time to love, and a time to hate;
>> a time of war, and a time of peace.

What profit hath he that worketh in that wherein he laboureth? I have seen the travail, which God hath given to the sons of men to be exercised in it. He hath made every thing beautiful in his time: also he hath set the world in their heart, so that no man can find out the work that God maketh from the beginning to the end. I know that there is no good in them, but for a man to rejoice, and to do good in his life. And also that every man should eat and drink, and enjoy the good of all his labour, it is the gift of God. I know that, whatsoever God doeth, it shall be for ever: nothing can be put to it, nor any thing taken from it: and God doeth it, that men should fear before him.

That which hath been is now;
    and that which is to be hath already been;
    and God requireth that which is past.

And moreover I saw under the sun the place of judgment, that wickedness was there; and the place of righteousness, that iniquity was there. I said in mine heart, God shall judge the righteous and the wicked: for there is a time there for every purpose and for every work.

I said in mine heart concerning the estate of the sons of men, that God might manifest them, and that they might see that they themselves are beasts. For that which befalleth the sons of men befalleth beasts; even one thing befalleth them: as the one dieth, so dieth the other; yea, they have all one breath; so that a man hath no preeminence above a beast: for all is vanity. All go unto one place; all are of the dust, and all turn to dust again. Who knoweth the spirit of man that goeth upward, and the spirit of the beast that goeth downward to the earth?

Wherefore I perceive that there is nothing better, than that a man should rejoice in his own works; for that is his portion: for who shall bring him to see what shall be after him?

OPPRESSION AND FOLLY
Ecclesiastes 4:1 – 5:9

So I returned, and considered all the oppressions that are done under the sun: and behold the tears of such as were oppressed, and they had no comforter; and on the side of their oppressors there was power; but they had no comforter. Wherefore I praised the dead which are already dead more than the living which are yet alive. Yea, better is he than both they, which hath not yet been, who hath not seen the evil work that is done under the sun.

Again, I considered all travail, and every right work, that for this a man is envied of his neighbour. This is also vanity and vexation of spirit.

The fool foldeth his hands together, and eateth his own flesh.
Better is an handful with quietness,
    than both the hands full with travail and vexation of spirit.

Then I returned, and I saw vanity under the sun.

There is one alone, and there is not a second;
    yea, he hath neither child nor brother:
yet is there no end of all his labour;
    neither is his eye satisfied with riches; neither saith he,
For whom do I labour, and bereave my soul of good?

This is also vanity, yea, it is a sore travail.

Two are better than one;
    because they have a good reward for their labour.
For if they fall, the one will lift up his fellow:
    but woe to him that is alone when he falleth;
    for he hath not another to help him up.
Again, if two lie together, then they have heat:
    but how can one be warm alone?
And if one prevail against him, two shall withstand him;
    and a threefold cord is not quickly broken.

Better is a poor and a wise child than an old and foolish king, who will no more be admonished. For out of prison he cometh to reign; whereas also he that is born in his kingdom becometh poor. I considered all the living which walk under the sun, with the second child that shall stand up in his stead. There is no end of all the people, even of all that have been before them: they also that come after shall not rejoice in him. Surely this also is vanity and vexation of spirit.

Keep thy foot when thou goest to the house of God, and be more ready to hear, than to give the sacrifice of fools: for they consider not that they do evil.

Be not rash with thy mouth,
  and let not thine heart be hasty to utter any thing before God:
  for God is in heaven, and thou upon earth:
  therefore let thy words be few.
For a dream cometh through the multitude of business;
  and a fool's voice is known by multitude of words.

When thou vowest a vow unto God, defer not to pay it; for he hath no pleasure in fools: pay that which thou hast vowed. Better is it that thou shouldest not vow, than that thou shouldest vow and not pay. Suffer not thy mouth to cause thy flesh to sin; neither say thou before the angel, that it was an error: wherefore should God be angry at thy voice, and destroy the work of thine hands? For in the multitude of dreams and many words there are also divers vanities: but fear thou God.

If thou seest the oppression of the poor, and violent perverting of judgment and justice in a province, marvel not at the matter: for he that is higher than the highest regardeth; and there be higher than they. Moreover the profit of the earth is for all: the king himself is served by the field.

THE DECEITFULNESS OF RICHES
Ecclesiastes 5:10 – 6:12

He that loveth silver shall not be satisfied with silver;
  nor he that loveth abundance with increase:
  this is also vanity.

When goods increase, they are increased that eat them:
  and what good is there to the owners thereof,
  saving the beholding of them with their eyes?

The sleep of a labouring man is sweet,
  whether he eat little or much:
  but the abundance of the rich will not suffer him to sleep.

There is a sore evil which I have seen under the sun, namely, riches kept for the owners thereof to their hurt. But those riches perish by evil travail: and he begetteth a son, and there is nothing in his hand.

As he came forth of his mother's womb,
    naked shall he return to go as he came,
and shall take nothing of his labour,
    which he may carry away in his hand.

And this also is a sore evil, that in all points as he came, so shall he go: and what profit hath he that hath laboured for the wind? All his days also he eateth in darkness, and he hath much sorrow and wrath with his sickness.

Behold that which I have seen: it is good and comely for one to eat and to drink, and to enjoy the good of all his labour that he taketh under the sun all the days of his life, which God giveth him: for it is his portion.

Every man also to whom God hath given riches and wealth, and hath given him power to eat thereof, and to take his portion, and to rejoice in his labour; this is the gift of God. For he shall not much remember the days of his life; because God answereth him in the joy of his heart.

There is an evil which I have seen under the sun, and it is common among men: A man to whom God hath given riches, wealth, and honour, so that he wanteth nothing for his soul of all that he desireth, yet God giveth him not power to eat thereof, but a stranger eateth it: this is vanity, and it is an evil disease.

If a man beget an hundred children, and live many years, so that the days of his years be many, and his soul be not filled with good, and also that he have no burial; I say, that an untimely birth is better than he. For he cometh in with vanity, and departeth in darkness, and his name shall be covered with darkness. Moreover he hath not seen the sun, nor known any thing: this hath more rest than the other. Yea, though he live a thousand years twice told, yet hath he seen no good: do not all go to one place?

All the labour of man is for his mouth,
    and yet the appetite is not filled.
For what hath the wise more than the fool?
    what hath the poor, that knoweth to walk before the living?
Better is the sight of the eyes than the wandering of the desire:
    this is also vanity and vexation of spirit.

That which hath been is named already,
  and it is known that it is man:
  neither may he contend with him that is mightier than he.
Seeing there be many things that increase vanity,
  what is man the better?

For who knoweth what is good for man in this life, all the days of his
vain life which he spendeth as a shadow? for who can tell a man what
shall be after him under the sun?

WISDOM AND JUDGMENT
Ecclesiastes 7:1 – 8:15

A good name is better than precious ointment;
  and the day of death than the day of one's birth.
It is better to go to the house of mourning,
  than to go to the house of feasting:
  for that is the end of all men;
  and the living will lay it to his heart.
Sorrow is better than laughter:
  for by the sadness of the countenance
  the heart is made better.
The heart of the wise is in the house of mourning;
  but the heart of fools is in the house of mirth.
It is better to hear the rebuke of the wise,
  than for a man to hear the song of fools.
For as the crackling of thorns under a pot,
  so is the laughter of the fool: this also is vanity.

Surely oppression maketh a wise man mad;
  and a gift destroyeth the heart.

Better is the end of a thing than the beginning thereof:
  and the patient in spirit is better than the proud in spirit.
Be not hasty in thy spirit to be angry:
  for anger resteth in the bosom of fools.

Say not thou, What is the cause that the former days
    were better than these?
    for thou dost not inquire wisely concerning this.

Wisdom is good with an inheritance:
    and by it there is profit to them that see the sun.
For wisdom is a defence, and money is a defence:
    but the excellency of knowledge is,
    that wisdom giveth life to them that have it.

Consider the work of God: for who can make that straight,
    which he hath made crooked?
In the day of prosperity be joyful,
    but in the day of adversity consider:
    God also hath set the one over against the other,
    to the end that man should find nothing after him.

All things have I seen in the days of my vanity: there is a just man that
perisheth in his righteousness, and there is a wicked man that
prolongeth his life in his wickedness. Be not righteous over much;
neither make thyself over wise: why shouldest thou destroy thyself?
Be not over much wicked, neither be thou foolish: why shouldest
thou die before thy time? It is good that thou shouldest take hold of
this; yea, also from this withdraw not thine hand: for he that feareth
God shall come forth of them all.

Wisdom strengtheneth the wise
    more than ten mighty men which are in the city.

For there is not a just man upon earth,
    that doeth good, and sinneth not.

Also take no heed unto all words that are spoken;
    lest thou hear thy servant curse thee:
For oftentimes also thine own heart knoweth
    that thou thyself likewise hast cursed others.

All this have I proved by wisdom: I said,

I will be wise; but it was far from me.
That which is far off, and exceeding deep, who can find it out?

I applied mine heart to know, and to search, and to seek out wisdom, and the reason of things, and to know the wickedness of folly, even of foolishness and madness: And I find more bitter than death the woman, whose heart is snares and nets, and her hands as bands: whoso pleaseth God shall escape from her; but the sinner shall be taken by her. Behold, this have I found, saith the preacher, counting one by one, to find out the account:

Which yet my soul seeketh, but I find not:
    one man among a thousand have I found;
    but a woman among all those have I not found.
Lo, this only have I found, that God hath made man upright;
    but they have sought out many inventions.

Who is as the wise man?
    and who knoweth the interpretation of a thing?
    a man's wisdom maketh his face to shine,
    and the boldness of his face shall be changed.

I counsel thee to keep the king's commandment,
    and that in regard of the oath of God.
Be not hasty to go out of his sight: stand not in an evil thing;
    for he doeth whatsoever pleaseth him.
Where the word of a king is, there is power:
    and who may say unto him, What doest thou?

Whoso keepeth the commandment shall feel no evil thing:
    and a wise man's heart discerneth both time and judgment.
Because to every purpose there is time and judgment,
    therefore the misery of man is great upon him.

For he knoweth not that which shall be:
    for who can tell him when it shall be?
There is no man that hath power over the spirit to retain the spirit;
    neither hath he power in the day of death:
    and there is no discharge in that war;
    neither shall wickedness deliver those that are given to it.

All this have I seen, and applied my heart unto every work that is done under the sun: there is a time wherein one man ruleth over another to his own hurt. And so I saw the wicked buried, who had come and gone from the place of the holy, and they were forgotten in the city where they had so done: this is also vanity.

Because sentence against an evil work is not executed speedily, therefore the heart of the sons of men is fully set in them to do evil. Though a sinner do evil an hundred times, and his days be prolonged, yet surely I know that it shall be well with them that fear God, which fear before him: But it shall not be well with the wicked, neither shall he prolong his days, which are as a shadow; because he feareth not before God.

There is a vanity which is done upon the earth; that there be just men, unto whom it happeneth according to the work of the wicked; again, there be wicked men, to whom it happeneth according to the work of the righteous: I said that this also is vanity. Then I commended mirth, because a man hath no better thing under the sun, than to eat, and to drink, and to be merry: for that shall abide with him of his labour the days of his life, which God giveth him under the sun.

THE CERTAINTY OF DEATH
Ecclesiastes 8:16 – 9:10

When I applied mine heart to know wisdom, and to see the business that is done upon the earth: (for also there is that neither day nor night seeth sleep with his eyes:) Then I beheld all the work of God, that a man cannot find out the work that is done under the sun: because though a man labour to seek it out, yet he shall not find it; yea further; though a wise man think to know it, yet shall he not be able to find it.

For all this I considered in my heart even to declare all this, that the righteous, and the wise, and their works, are in the hand of God: no man knoweth either love or hatred by all that is before them. All things come alike to all: there is one event to the righteous, and to the wicked; to the good and to the clean, and to the unclean; to him that sacrificeth, and to him that sacrificeth not: as is the good, so is the sinner; and he that sweareth, as he that feareth an oath.

This is an evil among all things that are done under the sun, that there is one event unto all: yea, also the heart of the sons of men is full of evil, and madness is in their heart while they live, and after that they go to the dead. For to him that is joined to all the living there is hope: for a living dog is better than a dead lion.

> For the living know that they shall die:
>> but the dead know not any thing,
>> neither have they any more a reward;
>> for the memory of them is forgotten.
> Also their love, and their hatred, and their envy, is now perished;
>> neither have they any more a portion for ever
>> in any thing that is done under the sun.

> Go thy way, eat thy bread with joy,
>> and drink thy wine with a merry heart;
>> for God now accepteth thy works.
> Let thy garments be always white;
>> and let thy head lack no ointment.

Live joyfully with the wife whom thou lovest all the days of the life of thy vanity, which he hath given thee under the sun, all the days of thy vanity: for that is thy portion in this life, and in thy labour which thou takest under the sun. Whatsoever thy hand findeth to do, do it with thy might; for there is no work, nor device, nor knowledge, nor wisdom, in the grave, whither thou goest.

TIME AND CHANCE
Ecclesiastes 9:11 – 11:6

I returned, and saw under the sun, that the race is not to the swift, nor the battle to the strong, neither yet bread to the wise, nor yet riches to men of understanding, nor yet favour to men of skill; but time and chance happeneth to them all. For man also knoweth not his time: as the fishes that are taken in an evil net, and as the birds that are caught in the snare; so are the sons of men snared in an evil time, when it falleth suddenly upon them.

This wisdom have I seen also under the sun, and it seemed great

unto me: There was a little city, and few men within it; and there came
a great king against it, and besieged it, and built great bulwarks against
it: Now there was found in it a poor wise man, and he by his wisdom
delivered the city; yet no man remembered that same poor man. Then
said I, Wisdom is better than strength: nevertheless the poor man's
wisdom is despised, and his words are not heard.

The words of wise men are heard in quiet
    more than the cry of him that ruleth among fools.
Wisdom is better than weapons of war:
    but one sinner destroyeth much good.

Dead flies cause the ointment of the apothecary
    to send forth a stinking savour:
    so doth a little folly him that is in reputation
    for wisdom and honour.

A wise man's heart is at his right hand;
    but a fool's heart at his left.
Yea also, when he that is a fool walketh by the way,
    his wisdom faileth him,
    and he saith to every one that he is a fool.

If the spirit of the ruler rise up against thee,
    leave not thy place; for yielding pacifieth great offences.

There is an evil which I have seen under the sun,
    as an error which proceedeth from the ruler:
Folly is set in great dignity, and the rich sit in low place.
I have seen servants upon horses,
    and princes walking as servants upon the earth.

He that diggeth a pit shall fall into it;
    and whoso breaketh an hedge, a serpent shall bite him.
Whoso removeth stones shall be hurt therewith;
    and he that cleaveth wood shall be endangered thereby.

If the iron be blunt, and he do not whet the edge,
    then must he put to more strength:
    but wisdom is profitable to direct.

Surely the serpent will bite without enchantment;
    and a babbler is no better.

The words of a wise man's mouth are gracious;
    but the lips of a fool will swallow up himself.
The beginning of the words of his mouth is foolishness:
    and the end of his talk is mischievous madness.
A fool also is full of words: a man cannot tell what shall be;
    and what shall be after him, who can tell him?

The labour of the foolish wearieth every one of them,
    because he knoweth not how to go to the city.

Woe to thee, O land, when thy king is a child,
    and thy princes eat in the morning!
Blessed art thou, O land, when thy king is the son of nobles,
    and thy princes eat in due season, for strength,
    and not for drunkenness!

By much slothfulness the building decayeth;
    and through idleness of the hands
    the house droppeth through.
A feast is made for laughter, and wine maketh merry:
    but money answereth all things.

Curse not the king, no not in thy thought;
    and curse not the rich in thy bedchamber:
for a bird of the air shall carry the voice,
    and that which hath wings shall tell the matter.

Cast thy bread upon the waters:
    for thou shalt find it after many days.
Give a portion to seven, and also to eight;
    for thou knowest not what evil shall be upon the earth.

If the clouds be full of rain, they empty themselves upon the earth:
    and if the tree fall toward the south, or toward the north,
    in the place where the tree falleth, there it shall be.
He that observeth the wind shall not sow;
    and he that regardeth the clouds shall not reap.

As thou knowest not what is the way of the spirit,
    nor how the bones do grow in the womb of her
    that is with child:
    even so thou knowest not the works of God who maketh all.

In the morning sow thy seed,
    and in the evening withhold not thine hand:
    for thou knowest not whether shall prosper,
    either this or that, or whether they both shall be alike good.

YOUTH AND OLD AGE
Ecclesiastes 11:7 – 12:8

Truly the light is sweet, and a pleasant thing it is for the eyes
    to behold the sun:
But if a man live many years, and rejoice in them all;
    yet let him remember the days of darkness;
    for they shall be many.
All that cometh is vanity.

Rejoice, O young man, in thy youth;
    and let thy heart cheer thee in the days of thy youth,
    and walk in the ways of thine heart,
    and in the sight of thine eyes: but know thou,
    that for all these things God will bring thee into judgment.
Therefore remove sorrow from thy heart,
    and put away evil from thy flesh:
    for childhood and youth are vanity.

Remember now thy Creator in the days of thy youth,
    while the evil days come not, nor the years draw nigh,
    when thou shalt say, I have no pleasure in them;
While the sun, or the light, or the moon, or the stars,
    be not darkened, nor the clouds return after the rain:
In the day when the keepers of the house shall tremble,
    and the strong men shall bow themselves,
    and the grinders cease because they are few,
    and those that look out of the windows be darkened,

And the doors shall be shut in the streets,
  when the sound of the grinding is low,
  and he shall rise up at the voice of the bird,
  and all the daughters of musick shall be brought low;
Also when they shall be afraid of that which is high,
  and fears shall be in the way,
  and the almond tree shall flourish,
  and the grasshopper shall be a burden,
  and desire shall fail:
  because man goeth to his long home,
  and the mourners go about the streets:
Or ever the silver cord be loosed,
  or the golden bowl be broken,
  or the pitcher be broken at the fountain,
  or the wheel broken at the cistern.
Then shall the dust return to the earth as it was:
  and the spirit shall return unto God who gave it.

Vanity of vanities, saith the preacher; all is vanity.

THE WHOLE DUTY OF MAN
Ecclesiastes 12:9–14

And moreover, because the preacher was wise, he still taught the people knowledge; yea, he gave good heed, and sought out, and set in order many proverbs. The preacher sought to find out acceptable words: and that which was written was upright, even words of truth.

The words of the wise are as goads, and as nails fastened by the masters of assemblies, which are given from one shepherd. And further, by these, my son, be admonished: of making many books there is no end; and much study is a weariness of the flesh.

Let us hear the conclusion of the whole matter:
Fear God, and keep his commandments:
  for this is the whole duty of man.
For God shall bring every work into judgment,
  with every secret thing, whether it be good,
  or whether it be evil.

Index of Primary Sources